Praise for
Coach Anyone About Anything . . .

"Unleashing your people to be the best they can be is the key to success in the decade ahead. This book strips the mystique out of coaching and will enable and empower you to help your team and your people get to the Future First."
—KEVIN ROBERTS, CEO Worldwide, Saatchi & Saatchi

"*Coach Anyone About Anything* is the most comprehensive coaching tool kit available. It is a clear, powerful coaching program for any coach regardless of your experience. This book gives you the practical, effective coaching tools necessary to help you and your players succeed. *Coach Anyone About Anything* will be a classic in the coaching field for years to come."
—IRIS HATFIELD, author of *A Question of Honesty*
and President, HuVista International

"On-point, insightful, inspiring, and actionable - what more could one seek from a comprehensive instruction book on coaching. I'm buying a copy for all of our consultants nationwide."
—CLIFFORD F. ESLINGER, Sr. Vice President,
Human Capital Consulting Group, Spherion Corporation

"*Coach Anyone About Anything* lasers through the sometimes fuzzy lines of coaching, management and leadership and delivers specific, comprehensive and revolutionary tools to immediately improve your effectiveness as a manager, parent, or trainer.
—BOBBI DEPORTER, author of *Quantum Learning, Quantum Business*

"The techniques and tools are practical, effective and easy to apply. If you want to empower others to achieve extraordinary success, read this book now!"
—JERRY GAUCHE, Vice President, Organizational Effectiveness,
National OilWell, Inc.

"Takes the cloak off of many management and leadership mysteries and shows why coaching is the motivational, get-it-done method for tomorrow's work environment. Insightful, thought-provoking ideas that apply to all walks of life. A must read for tomorrow's coaches."
—DAVID A. STONEBARGER, Director, Human Resources, Dresser-Rand Company

"*Coach Anyone About Anything* provides a wide variety of practical recipes for coaches to use in 'facilitating people in their own commitment and enthusiasm to accomplish their objectives'."
—MARY BETH MOEHRING, Vice President,
Training & Organizational Development, SYSCO Corporation

"This book is different! At last, a book that clearly explains what Coaching is and, more importantly, how it can be applied in 'real situations'. Improve your life now - buy it!"
—GORDON A. HEADLEY, Head of Global Breakthrough Performance, LASMO plc, London, England

"In coaching my leadership team, we developed actions that drove revenues from $90M to $180M in four years. Currently, I live and work in Singapore managing another Asia Pacific business. I find these coaching techniques as applicable in Asia Pacific as they are in the USA to drive business growth.
—JIM HEALY, Vice President & General Manager, Asia Pacific

"The most powerful economic unit in the new millennium is the individual entrepreneur...not the firm. The key to unleashing the entrepreneur's full power is coaching...at last, a road map!"
—TED ZOUZOUNIS, CLU, Partner, D/A Financial Group of California

"*Coach Anyone About Anything* is a must read for all who manage other people. Directing others to get the job done accomplishes just that. Effective coaching can motivate and inspire others to not only get it done, but to achieve top performance."
—JEFFREY R. BLAND, Senior Director, People Services, RadioShack Corporation

"The authors deliver a powerful message to solving complex issues with practical models ready for easy implementation that will unleash the untapped power of the people of your organization to attain new heights."
—RICK O'NEIL, President, Help-U-Sell Corporation

"*Coach Anyone About Anything* presents a brilliant, wise and extremely useful model for developing coaching skills. The authors present very practical examples and activities applicable by managers, and parents, in any culture who want to create now, the organizations of the future."
—ROBERTO HERRERA, Director of Affiliated Companies, CEMEX, Mexico

"Already seasoned executive coaches, we enhanced our abilities with what we found in "Coach Anyone". We recommend this book to anyone who wants to dramatically improve their coaching effectiveness and produce breakthrough results."
—SHIDEH SEDGH BINA & MICHAEL WALDMAN,Senior Partners, INSIGNIAM Performance Consulting

"Calling on readers to intentionally operate from a coaching stance, *Coach Anyone About Anything* outlines an approach that ensures a positive result through creating and sustaining a powerful coaching relationship."
—GAIL HUGHES, Vice President, Organization Capability, Chevy Chase Bank

"Executives and managers have become acutely aware that as hard as leadership and management skills are to acquire and apply, today's employees demand more. Coaching is the vital link between establishing a vision, marshalling resources toward common goals, and truly getting unexpectedly high performance from your team. The good news of *Coach Anyone About Anything* is that this critical skill can be learned thanks to the insights from these two talented authors."
—BRIAN E. FALCK, President & CEO, H. J. Heinz Company of Canada Ltd

"... a way to train my 4th grade students to think more like coaches. They are excelling in coaching each other on a daily basis."
—PAULA KING, educator

"Working in the UK financial services market, we have successfully used the methodology that Germaine and Jed introduced to us. It translates into our personal lives as well. Coaching with a bit of humour helps the medicine go down and, they surely have a wicked sense of humour!"
—NIGEL A. DYER, FCII and JUDY KELLIE
Intelligent Marketing Partnership, England

"I find a lot of repackaging of old management training being called and sold as coaching. Not in this book! Here, you'll find that Germaine and Jed have defined the art and science of real coaching for business and personal life. With their help, my executive coaching practice has leapt to the next level."
—MICHAEL A. TATE, Life and Leadership Coach, Vantage Associates, Inc.

"I now feel confident that in making *Coach Anyone About Anything* a required reading, our management team will absorb the fundamentals of the leadership style I want to convey to all members of our staff."
—MARC LANDRY, Chairman of the Board, President
and CEO, Go Figure Technology, Inc.

"Anyone working with people, children, subordinates or bosses should read this book. The chapter dealing with the differences among coaching, management and leadership is worth the cost of the book."
—CARL E. KING, Major, USMC Retired, President and CEO,
Insights Corporate Selection Systems Inc.

"Not everyone can be Vince Lombardi or Joe Paterno, but for an excellent, powerful and very user-friendly set of guidelines to head you in that direction, *Coach Anyone About Anything* is hard to beat."
—MICK FLEMING, Attorney, Lane, Powell, Spears, Lubersky,
and Owner, KidsCentre Childcare

"Jed and Germaine can coach anyone about anything. With this fresh approach to an old, but increasingly critical skill, everyone can re-enforce and upgrade this highly valued skill by reading this book.
—ART WILSON, CEO of Critical Path Strategies, Inc.

COACH
ANYONE
ABOUT
ANYTHING

COACH ANYONE ABOUT ANYTHING

How to Help People Succeed in Business and Life

BY GERMAINE PORCHÉ AND JED NIEDERER

The Eagle's View® Company

1st Edition Copyright © 2001 by Germaine Porché and Jed Niederer
Wharton Publishing, Inc.
#210 2683 Via De La Valle, Suite G
Del Mar, California 92014

2nd Edition
The Eagle's View Company
P. O. Box 6154
Kingwood, TX 77325

Printed in the United States of America 2001, 2003, 2007, 2009, 2010

Cover and interior design: Robert Aulicino/www.aulicinodesign.com

Porché, Germaine
    Coach anyone about anything : how to help people
    succeed in business and life / by Germaine Porché and
    Jed Niederer. -- 1st ed. 2nd ed.
        p. cm.
    Includes bibliographical references and index.
    ISBN: 978-0-9826-6040-9
    Library of Congress Control Number: 2010923006

ACKNOWLEDGMENTS

This book is an acknowledgment of our families, friends, coaches, and clients.

Without God's help, reassurance, and coaching, this book would not have been possible.

We, Jed and Germaine, would like to personally and publicly thank each other for a devotion to coaching that transcends the concepts of what partners are in life, marriage, and business.

Special and grateful acknowledgment to Germaine's mother and father, Clydia and Charles Porché. "Thanks, Mom and Dad, for a wonderful life and for my eight brothers and sisters and their families, who coached me and taught me how to coach."

In memory of Jed's father, Edward Niederer, Jr., and his mothers, Esther Worrell Niederer and Betta Elliott Niederer. "Thanks to my four sisters and their families, who all have coached me and taught me how to coach."

Thanks, also, to
Our publisher, Dale Strack, Wharton Publishing

Our editors, Eva Shaw, Ph.D., and Jacquelyn Landis
Deirdre Frontczak, Ph.D.
Tina LoSasso
Our designer: Robert Aulicino

American University/National Training Laboratories, Washington, D.C., Class #29 and all of Germaine's professors and former Director of the Program, Dr. Al Cooke.

Cindy Angelly
Christopher Bernal, M.S.
Miguel Bernal, Ph.D.

Cascade Natural Gas Corporation, Seattle, WA
Richard L. Benson
William J. Broussard, Ph.D.
Robert B. Chapman, Ph.D.
Jackie Comola, M.S.
Alan C. Davidson, CLU
Bobbi DePorter
Donald J. DePorter
Werner Erhard
Cliff & Elaine Eslinger
Geoff Furtney
Jerry & Cathy Gauche
Wilton J. and Celine Guillory
Ernie Herbert
Greg Hill
Paul Hottle, M. S.
Tex & Gail Johnston and Family
Michael P. King
Carl & Paula King
Stuart & Cece Kirsner
Larry J. Lamb
Landmark Education, San Francisco, CA
Pat & Bob Lindgren
Joanie Mattson
Mike Morton
Richard Tanner Pascale, Ph.D.
Don Pearson
Nolan & Peggy Rome
Jerry Rose
Doug Saam
Laurie Seekamp Sanderson
Terry Sierakowski
Herb Tanzer & Beth Goodman
Michael A. Tate
Judi Weir
Art Wilson
Theodore Zouzounis, CLU
Bill & Judy Topkis

Epigraph

Go to the people,
Learn from them, love them.
Start with what they know,
Build on what they have.
But the best of leaders, when their task is accomplished
and their work is done,
"We have done it ourselves," the people will all remark.
—Chinese poem, 23 B.C.

Coach Anyone About Anything

CONTENTS

Introduction

*"In the 21st century, organizations have to achieve peak performance...
by unleashing the power of people—not by leading them, not by
managing them, but by inspiring them."*
—Kevin Roberts, CEO
Saatchi & Saatchi (*Fast Company*, September 2000)

coach´-ing: facilitating people in their own commitment and
enthusiasm to accomplish their objectives.

Everyone can be a coach to help others. Everyone can experience
improvement in life through the help of a caring, resourceful and focused
coach. Coaching is simple, it's effective, and it's applicable to a dozen
areas of life.

This book is written for you with practical information, whether you're
coaching an individual, a business team, or a volunteer group. It's written for professional coaches and for parents.

In this book, you'll get proven methods to boost your skills as a coach.
We're going to share with you tools, exercises, and processes that we've
invented to help you accomplish your coaching objectives and dreams.
After finishing this book, you'll come away with the most complete coaching toolkit available today.

Included in the book is A Coaching Architecture, a one-year timeline
marking the important steps, phases, and junctures appropriate to most
coaching scenarios. It's at the end of this introduction along with a
description of each part. It also references the book's chapter(s) for more
in-depth information.

You'll also find at the end of this book the Coaching Tools & Models
Index, naming 56 valuable coaching tools and techniques described in
this book. The Coaching Tools & Models Index is a valuable tool in itself.

Have you ever wondered how coaching differs from management or
leadership? We've discovered that most businesspeople can't articulate
the difference. In this book, you'll gain a clear and powerful understand-

ing of the differences between coaching, management, and leadership so you can know when to coach, manage, or lead. Most executives and managers don't know. Some teachers, corporate leaders, and volunteers find the lines too fuzzy, and this book gives specific help. Parents are walking that coaching, management, and leadership road and wondering if they're even going the right direction. This book's information-dense text helps parents, too.

In Chapter 5, we're going to share with you a revolutionary perspective about coaching. People aren't coachable! Did you just say, "Oh, no!"? Take heart, this discovery will dramatically improve your coaching ability. With the tips in Chapter 5, you'll learn how this discovery can free you from unnecessary stress and immediately enhance your coaching effectiveness.

Learn the four key player attributes: knowledge, skill, confidence, and motivation. Find out how to positively impact them and improve your players' results in Chapter 6.

Coaches should only ask questions, right? Read Chapter 4, The Coaching Scope, and then see what you think. Coaches should never give advice, right? Again, see Chapter 4.

Ever wonder when to talk and when to listen? Sure, you do. Coaches do, too. We'll give you a graphic guide to help you, the coach, answer that question. See Chapter 6 for The Coaching Spectrum.

By the way, while you're reading, we intend for you to develop or polish your own Coaching Philosophy. Although this will happen quite naturally for you, Chapter 8 will give you some great tips to create Your Coaching Philosophy, a vital tool for any coach to have. You'll learn the system by which players rate their coaches. And we'll share with you the phenomenon we've discovered that we call the "value drift." It's a little-recognized and usually invisible force, always working against the coach—whether veteran or novice, at work or at home. Find out how to see it working in your player and how to use it to your advantage in Chapter 9.

Chapter 13 gives you a tool unequaled in its facility to gain access to what is immediately on your clients' minds with regard to their dreams and objectives–the DreamMakers & DreamBrakers Audit. What things are propelling them to achieve their goals, and what things are impeding them? Don't miss Chapter 13!

The telephone has been around for over a century, yet most of us don't know some basic guidelines for how to use it most effectively, especially in coaching situations. As a result, it may seem like an inappropriate coaching tool. Yet the telephone can be very effective and save countless prime-time hours to invest elsewhere. For the commuting parent or caring adult relative who wants to stay connected and make a difference with teens and children time zones away, the telephone may be the only medium available. See Chapter 15 to find out how you can be an effective coach by phone.

Coaching teams? Although nearly all of the coaching concepts presented here can be applied to teams, we have a special chapter with some unique tools to help you guide teams to success, Chapter 14.

Need a fast way to get a handle on what your player's/client's business is all about? See Chapters 11 and 12. Chapter 11 offers a list of incisive questions to gain the understanding you desire to effectively coach your business client. Chapter 12 illustrates an interactive process to enable you and your client to learn about his or her organization even more profoundly.

For those of you who want to know how to get started in coaching as a profession or further build your clientele, see Chapter 16, How to Begin and Build Your Coaching Business. Here, we provide some marvelous networking and prospecting tools and ways to answer every prospective player's/client's three questions: Why coaching? Why you? and Why now? You'll also discover that the coaching profession has some inherent qualities that help you grow your clientele like no other.

In our final chapter, Patience and Power, we examine power itself and how it applies to the privilege of coaching. Then we tie the book together by illustrating uses for all the coaching tools we've given you in this single chapter.

Finally, we'll give you our Coaching Inventory, both a self-assessment and a learning tool. It is designed to review, and in some instances, introduce 55 key coaching principles, structures, practices, and approaches. It allows you to assess your coaching ability.

Whether you're coaching a work team or your child's soccer team, the techniques we share in this book will improve your effectiveness. Regardless of your experience level as a coach, the keys we are about to share with you will unlock your natural coaching ability.

Maybe coaching is new to you or you haven't thought of its importance before. Are you aware that we've all coached at one time or another? Have you helped a colleague figure out a tricky problem? Have you been involved in a community project or a fundraising event? Have you worked with or headed a team in the office?

If you've been coached at one time in your life—and trust us, you have, although you may not have called it that—you already have a handle about what works and what might not be effective.

May we coach you?

May we help you become a better coach to assist anyone to succeed at anything?

If you want to be a more successful leader, supporter, and team member, your answer will be yes.

This book is the result of our professional work as coaches. It's also part of our personal involvement on volunteer, community, and educational projects.

We've given workshops, seminars, sessions, and one-on-one programs to people in every facet of life, from educational leadership to men and women entering new career pathways. The term "coach" might be new to you, but we've been studying and testing various coaching styles and techniques for more than 30 cumulative years. As you read the following pages, we hope you will experience personal insights or "ah-ha's." We call them Thunderbolts!, a term our friend, Alan C. Davidson, CLU, used to describe our work.

Thunderbolts! are insights that are so revealing and powerful that you might smack your forehead with the heel of your hand and say, "Whew, that's incredible!" These enable you to be a more useful and helpful coach and enhance your coaching ability.

Even though we'll focus most of our attention on the work environment, don't be surprised if you experience personal breakthroughs in your role as a parent, spouse, or friend, as well.

This book is written for everyone. It's for the executive in the boardroom, the parent coaching a teenager, the entrepreneur motivating clients, the corporate trainer, the human resource professional, the little league coach, and the friend who lends an ear.

In this book, we'll be using new terms or words in ways that might be unfamiliar to you. We'll define them immediately. For instance, we call the person receiving your coaching "the player." If you are coaching a sports team, then this certainly makes sense. And it also makes sense when coaching a business team member or a client. He or she must participate and perform; thus, he or she is a player.

The examples and case histories presented in this book are real life examples. Consistent with our commitment to client confidentiality, names, titles, and companies have, in most cases, been changed or omitted.

What will you find in this book? Within these pages you'll

- take the mystery out of coaching.
- erase the notion or myth that coaching is difficult.
- discover essential and proven coaching principles.
- experience the magnificence of others (and yourself).
- use coaching models and tools.
- say, "I can do this! I can coach!"

If you've already flipped through this book (yes, we do that, too), we urge you to read the old-fashioned, linear way, starting at the beginning. You'll find that works best. This is true whether you've been a coach for years or this is your first experience. The material is sequential, and you'll build on the information from the previous parts to use the techniques presented later.

No need to wait. It's time to unlock your natural coaching ability and gain your coach's edge.

—Germaine Porché & Jed Niederer

A COACHING ARCHITECTURE

(Descriptions below refer to the numbered items in the graphic –
A Coaching Architecture.)

1. Present Coaching Biography — The coach asks his or her player/client or potential player/client to read the coach's Coaching Biography. The biography's purpose is to help establish the coach's credibility and build rapport with the player. (See Chapter 8.)

2. Introduce Outcomes Contract — The coach introduces to the player the concept of contracting for outcomes in the coach/player relationship. The coach explains the 10 points of the typical Coaching Outcomes Contract. At this juncture, the outcomes contract serves as a "discussion document" to help develop the foundation of the coach/player relationship. (See Chapter 3.)

3. Complete Eagle's View Inventory or Personal Effectiveness Checklist — The coach asks the player to complete the Eagle's View Inventory or the coach asks the player to answer the 18 questions of the Personal Effectiveness Checklist. The purpose here is to become familiar with the player's sense of his or her personal effectiveness. It can signal for the coach possible areas in which she or he can assist the player in their productivity. (See Chapter 11.)

4. Client says "Yes" to Contract Terms — The player and the coach agree, in principle and spirit, to the first draft of the Coaching Outcomes Contract. (See Chapter 3.)

5. Schedule Regular Coaching Sessions — The coach and player schedule regular coaching sessions – for example: one hour per week, the same time each week. (See Chapters 2 and 3.)

6. Compare Client Objectives to Futurability Checklist —The coach and player compare the player's objectives to The Futurability for Objectives Checklist. This is to ensure that the player's objectives are not just "wishes" and "hopes," but rather realizable achievements that both player and coach are committed to accomplishing. (See Chapter 3.)

7. Finalize Outcomes Contract — The player and coach agree upon and sign the Coaching Outcomes Contract. (See Chapter 3.)

8. Behavioral Styles Profile — The coach asks the player to complete a Behavioral Styles Profile*, the results of which can help the coach determine the best coaching tactical approaches with this player.

9. Provide E-mail & Voice Mail Protocols — The coach provides the player with the E-mail Checklist and the Voice Mail Protocol. (See Chapters 3 and 15.)

10. Force Rank Things that Motivate — The coach asks the player to "force rank" the Five Things That Motivate. (See Chapter 6.)

11. How to Get the Most Out of the Coach — The coach gives the player Ten Ways to Get the Most From Your Coach. (See Chapter 5.)

12. Learn Client's Business, 32 Questions — The coach proceeds to learn the player's/client's business utilizing the Learning Your Client's Business – 32 Questions. (See Chapter 11.)

13. DreamMakers & DreamBrakers Audit — The coach asks the player to complete the DreamMakers & DreamBrakers Audit to determine the weight, lift, drag and thrust the player experiences on their achievement flight path. (See Chapter 13.)

14. Coaching Inventory (self-assessment) — The coach completes the Coaching Inventory to assess their coaching ability and design a way forward. (See Chapter 17.)

15. Quarterly Milestones Review — This review is intended to determine whether the promised intended results of the player are being achieved. The particular milestones have been described in the outcomes contract. The player and coach generate action plans from the future. (See Chapters 2 and 3.)

16. Year-End Completion, Accomplishment & Celebration — This is a time for completing the past, acknowledging the player's accom-

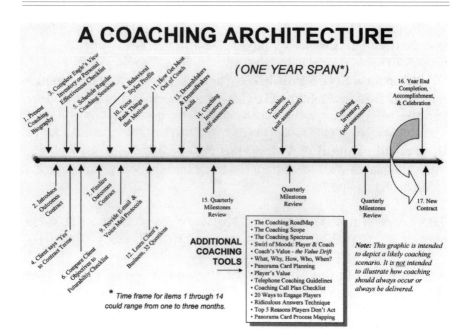

A COACHING ARCHITECTURE

(ONE YEAR SPAN*)

Note: This graphic is intended to depict a likely coaching scenario. It is not intended to illustrate how coaching should always occur or always be delivered.

* Time frame for items 1 through 14 could range from one to three months.

plishments, and celebrating them. It is also a time for planning the future standing on the foundation of this past year's accomplishments. (See Chapter 3.)

17. New Contract — The player, pleased with the past year's results, and the coach agree to continue their coach/player relationship. They create a new Coaching Outcomes Contract for the coming year. (See Chapter 3.)

* There are numerous behavioral styles profiles and assessments available today. The authors have used a wide variety of these and do not endorse any in particular. Several have proven to be quite helpful for coaching engagements.

Start at the beginning and read straight to the end. Good advice.

However, we won't be dismayed if you flip through, read the quotes, digest the models, and refer to the material at the end. You may want to read the quotes and case studies and scan the Table of Contents and Index. We hope you'll browse through the Bibliography because we've included some of the books we've found to be most helpful.

At the beginning of every chapter, we've included the "Outcomes of this chapter." This is a fast-track guide that gives you a quick overview, and of course, there's much more within the chapters to learn.

Dr. Georgi Lozanov, the father of accelerated learning, discovered that baroque music makes learning easier. He found that it relaxes you and, at the same time, leaves your mind alert and able to concentrate. Composers such as Bach, Mozart, Vivaldi, and Handel used very specific beats and patterns that automatically synchronize our minds with our bodies. While studying new material, baroque music awakens the intuitive, creative right brain so that its input can be integrated into the whole process. Therefore, we suggest that you play this music in the background while you read this book and especially when you complete the exercises outlined.

Remember, you can share this book with your colleagues, co-workers, and kids. It's written for everyone who wants to help others succeed at anything.

If you have some coaching experience, then you may want to take the Coaching Inventory, found in Chapter 17, before reading the book. Once you finish and have applied the material, we hope you'll reassess your coaching skills.

We'd appreciate hearing from you and learning of your coaching experiences. Please contact us at Eagle's View Systems, 1525 Lakeville Drive, Suite 127, Kingwood, TX 77339, or through our website at http://www.eaglesview.com, or by phone at 281-348-9181 or 888-387-9786.

The Coach's Edge

- **C — Committed.** Be authentically committed to the player achieving his or her objectives.

- **O — Outcomes.** Have a written Outcomes Contract.

- **A — Ask.** Tend to ask questions rather than tell the player what to do or give solutions/answers.
  (What? Why? How? Who? When?)

- **C — Coachable.** Remember players are generally <u>not</u> coachable and have moments of being able to be coached.

- **H — Harness.** Harness and direct your energies with a powerful, personal Coaching Philosophy.

- **S — Spectrum.** Use the Coaching Spectrum (Assess the player's mood, knowledge, skill, confidence, and motivation.)

- **E — Enthusiasm.** Facilitate the player's own enthusiasm and commitment to accomplish his or her objectives, keeping in mind his or her Thunderbolt! vision.

- **D — Dialogue.** Coach the dialogue in the pathway to the player's intended results.

- **G — Go for it!** Ask more of the player than he or she would ask of themselves. Invite the player to "go for it!" and achieve Thunderbolt!

- **E — Every.** Every time you coach, ask permission.

CHAPTER 1

To lead the people, walk behind them.
—Lao-Tzu

THE COACHING ROLE

Outcomes of this chapter:
- Bust the myth: "Coaching is difficult."
- Distinguish coaching from leadership and management.
- Learn when advice is coaching and when it isn't.

You may have heard this axiom: Everyone's a coach.

Well, it's true. Even though you may never have thought of yourself in this way before, you definitely have had coaching experience.

The best news yet is you already know and use a number of coaching tools. You already have coaching skills.

What you'll find in this book, through the case studies and experiences, is information to become more effective at coaching.

Still can't imagine how you could be considered a coach? Have you helped or assisted friends, co-workers, "direct-reports," youngsters, or an entire soccer team? If the answer is yes, you are a coach.

We're about to expose the myth that coaching is difficult and mysterious. Here's a Thunderbolt!, coaching can be easy and straightforward.

Yes, there are ways to make it complicated, but there are also tricks to this trade. Besides, if you're more than five years old, you've probably had on-the-job experience as both a coach and a player. To be truly effective and genuinely assist others, you will want the methods we're giving you. And take these methods in the spirit in which we intend them: not hard and fast rules for everyone, but strategies worth trying.

*Anyone who stops learning is old, whether at twenty or eighty. Anyone
who keeps learning stays young.*
—Henry Ford

We are committed that you will complete this book with an "attitude." What we mean is that you'll have an attitude about coaching that says, "I can do this." If you begin with this attitude, you will gain new insights and be able to use the tools that add thrust to your coaching endeavors and expand your coaching ability.

Further, the more you learn about yourself and how human beings relate to coaching, the better your coaching results will be. One of the most important things we have discovered is that as people, while we may look and often act in dissimilar ways, we have our humanity in common.

Our humanity rests upon a series of learned behaviors, woven together into patterns that are infinitely fragile and never directly inherited.
—Margaret Mead, *Male and Female*

As you practice these principles of coaching, you will begin to discover and celebrate the brilliance of others' and your own magnificence, as well. After our CoachLabs, participants report that they realize the profound privilege and honor it is to coach people.

To be able to work with people through both good and difficult times, accomplishing great things, has led us places that we never thought we'd go. We'll get you there, too, through the use of simple, but effective tools designed to uncover the obstacles that stop players from accomplishing their goals. We've seen this happen time and again. We promise that your coaching toolkit will be filled when you finish this book.

Once your mind is stretched by a new idea, it will never again return to its original size.
—Oliver Wendell Holmes

You're a Coach

Remember learning to tie your shoestrings? Or have you recently taught your child to do so?

The coordination and the patience required to finish that task seemed overwhelming at the time, right? By sticking with it, you achieved the goal. Finally, there was a perfect bow.

Think back. Can you remember the person who was equally patient with you and taught you how to tie your shoestrings? Germaine recalls, "It was my mom. She was a fabulous coach. I felt so accomplished. I'll never forget that feeling and her smile." Coaches feel pride when a player succeeds. You will, too.

Yes, whoever encouraged you to tie your shoestrings was your coach. That person watched what you were doing and coached you through it.

Executives and managers we meet continue to tell us that they "don't feel fully competent" in the coaching arena. They say they know coaching isn't really training. They realize command and control are generally inappropriate for coaching, while remaining legitimate and effective tools for managing and leading.

Lee McKay, president and CEO for a telemarketing company based in Boca Raton, Florida, attended one of our CoachLabs and asked this question: "I can take control. I can command. But tell me quickly: Are there similarly powerful tools for coaching?"

Absolutely; we guarantee it.

Distinguishing Coaching from Leadership and Management

Here's a pop quiz: What's the difference between coaching and leadership and management?

Try this exercise. (You'll need something on which to write.)

Everybody knows a great leader. If we're fortunate, we may have worked with one. It could be that someone has complimented our own leadership skills.

Take a moment and jot down your thoughts to this question: What is leadership?

Great. Now think of someone you respect who has managed a situation or company well. Write your thoughts to this question: What is management?

Finally, the last question: What is coaching? What comes to mind on this topic? Put your thoughts down.

Don't feel glum. If you were unable to immediately identify the definitions and make distinctions from the characteristics above, you're actually in great company. Few people can. However, when you understand the differences, you will have a clear picture of each. From this information, you choose the role you'll need to play. Keep in mind that regardless of whom you're coaching, you may have to switch roles with lightning speed. We've found this in our consulting business and know you will, too.

Now look back at your notes. Do you see any similarities among the three areas? If you're like most people, you'll notice what you've written could apply to all three areas, except there are contrasts.

Don't be shocked if this exercise leads you to question yourself and your role as a leader, manager, and/or coach. Are you managing when you should be coaching, or vice versa? And are you leading when coaching would be more effective? Are you confused about the boundaries of each?

You can look for definitions in your trusty Webster's, but these are how we define the three roles:

lead-er-ship: declaring a future and enrolling people into making that future happen.

man-age-ment: coordinating people and materials to accomplish specific milestones/objectives, which will make the declared future happen.

coach-ing: facilitating people in their own commitment and enthusiasm to accomplish their objectives.

Enthusiasm is the inspiration that makes you 'wake up and live.' It puts spring in your step, spring in your heart, a twinkle in your eyes, confidence in yourself and your fellowmen.
—Author Unknown

Now that you've reviewed the three definitions, notice that coaching, leadership, and management are all a matter of context or being. They are not a matter of content or doing. All three may even do the same things at times, but the context determines the outcome. Are you being a leader, manager, or coach? Here's another view seen in a leading business publication: Generation X is poised to reshape the business world, and says one young researcher, "Woe be to the companies that don't embrace the new workplace dynamic." Bruce Tulgan is a former Wall Street lawyer turned one of America's foremost experts on Generation X. His company is

Rainmaker Thinking, Inc.; his book is *Managing Generation X*. Tulgan responds to the question: How do you keep people who are inclined to walk away at a moment's notice? "You need to turn managers into coaches, and you need to start negotiating with people on a day-to-day, week-to-week basis and make 'pay for performance' a reality, not just a slogan."

Cliff Thurston, an executive with a delivery service in the Midwest, was in one of our CoachLabs. Cliff asked a question that might be on your mind: How do I know when I'm managing and should be leading?

Many executives have no clear boundaries between the roles. They, too, often manage when they should be leading. What's happening, however, is that they're managing the operations of the company instead of creating the vision for the company and allowing subordinates to step into that vision.

Once executives realize that they may be negatively affecting the progress of their companies, they step back. They begin to apply the skills that best suit their leadership role, that of the visionary. They grow the business by having others do the hands-on job of operating the company. Said another way, they let the managers manage.

Leaders and managers coach their players by switching attention from the activity to the player. With attention in this direction, they work with the player and the goals that the player is committed to accomplishing. Notice they don't oversee or manage the player while coaching. Rather, they ask questions, provide information or share philosophies and methodologies, and observe the process.

That's All? Not Quite.

From experience, we've learned that when we tell players what to do, it not only strips their personal power, it robs them of taking responsibility for the choice that was made.

Let's say you're coaching your daughter's softball team. It's the bottom of the ninth. You gather the ten-year-olds together and say, "Okay, Emily, Tyler, Courtney, when you get up to the plate, swing at every pitch." All should go well except that the other team's coach sticks in a substitute pitcher. This child's pitches are the wildest you've ever seen. We're talking about the ones that barely make it out of her hands before they plunk to the dirt. Or at the speed of light, they head toward the hitter and then abruptly, as if propelled by rocket fuel, careen toward the parking lot. Goodness...is that your brand new car the ball's headed for?

As the scenario continues, the players do exactly what they've been told by their coach. Within minutes, the wild pitches have struck out three of your best players. Who is responsible?

Now take this into your business arena. It doesn't matter that you aren't an expert in the player's area of expertise. The point is that when you—the coach—tell the player what to do and the objective isn't met, he or she has been relieved of all responsibility. That's definitely not coaching. That's the antiquated do-as-I-say style of management. It didn't work all that well in the prehistoric age, and it's even less effective today. That's why coaching skills are so valuable.

And One More Thing...

We suggest that you begin to think like a coach and create in yourself the type of coach you wish you could have had. Learn to recognize the applications for leadership, management, and coaching opportunities. Remember, coaching is about the other person. The spotlight is on your player.

In the next chapter, we'll look at coaching styles, how activity and action are diverse yet similar, and how to build a strong foundation for your coaching skills.

CHAPTER 2

Things go rushing by us at an accelerated speed, getting more and more complex. We can't get hold of it. It's too complicated. It's moving too fast. So we create a vision of what we want it (the future) to look like... Then that vision instructs us backwards in how to get there. The vision sorts out our decisions.
—John Naisbitt, *Megatrends 2000*

WHAT ARE YOU COACHING?

Outcomes of this chapter:
- Utilize a coaching dialogue.
- Understand activity versus action.
- Discover a strong foundation for your coaching skills.

Congratulations. Someone has asked you to be a coach. This could be a friend, a colleague, or a group from your volunteer organization. This person may be your client. You're feeling great and rightly so.

By the time the initial conversation with your player is over, odds are that you have an idea about what the player is up to. No doubt you're feeling jam-packed with so much knowledge and experience that you are eager to share it all with this new client.

Exactly what will you coach? Before you answer, give this question some thought. There's no right answer, but we urge you to think the relationship through so that you can provide the best information and coaching and make it accessible and effective for your player.

In this chapter, you'll learn what a coach coaches. You'll become familiar with new coaching models: the "Go the Distance!" model and the "Activity vs. Action" model. By the end of this chapter, you will have a strong foundation in coaching, and you'll know where to focus and what to emphasize as a coach.

The "Go the Distance!" Coaching Model

Let's get back to the question, What are you coaching?

Many people have come to us over the years to learn how to be effective coaches. They have fears or hesitation about getting too personally involved with people.

After a large seminar in Kansas City, Kelly Kasslebaum, who was starting his third lifetime career and recently received an MBA, came up to us and said, "I want to coach people in their business, and I'm not interested in what's happening with their marriage, significant other, etc. I just want to concentrate on business and nothing else. Am I being reasonable?"

Kelly had a valid question. Others want to coach only in relationships, telling people how to get along better or how to develop more powerful personal relationships, etc. They want to coach personal relationships and prefer not to deal with business because they (the coaches) are not knowledgeable about the player's business.

The truth is that you're not coaching a business or a relationship. You're coaching the dialogue in the pathway to the player's intended results, whether that's personal or business.

Please look at the Go the Distance! model for clarity about what we mean. (See Figure 1.) The right side of the model has the vertical axis rep-

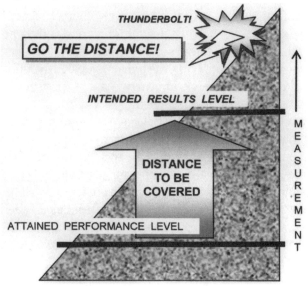

Figure 1.

resenting measurement. By measurement, we're referring to the continuum of results that the player can produce or is committed to produce.

The bold horizontal lines represent the levels of results where the player is located:

Attained Performance Level is the level that the player has already achieved. The player does not need coaching in this area because the results at this level have already been achieved. This isn't the best use of coaching time to try to coach at this level.

Intended Results Level is what the player is committed to producing. The more clear the player is about the results that he or she would like to produce, the more value will be received from each coaching session.

In a coaching relationship, clarity is key in developing the intended results that the player is committed to producing. Clarity, which is ensured by the coach, must be taken to the point that there isn't any question in the player's or coach's mind about what the intended results are.

Here are some questions to ask at the beginning of every coaching relationship. You'll want to modify the questions as they pertain to teams, entrepreneurs, teenagers, and volunteers. Be sure to write down the questions and the answers. This isn't the type of material to leave to your memory, even if it's never failed you.

- What are the results to be produced? Results should be quantified as much as possible. By this, we mean results written in %, #, $, increase or decrease amounts, etc.
- What is the specific timeframe to produce the intended results? Have your player be specific. You may have to ask several questions to get this information.
- What obstacles can prohibit the player from producing the intended results? Real or imagined obstacles should be noted.
- What does the player have at stake, or what are the risks if the intended results are not produced?
- Is the player committed? Does the player promise to produce the results, or are the results wishful thinking?
- Is the player supported by key people in his or her environment to produce the intended results? How is the player supported?
- Who in the player's environment would like to see the project or player fail?

During one of our CoachLabs, participant and sales vice-president Graham Weatherly asked for coaching. Graham described the situation: "I'm attempting to coach two of my regional sales managers in Europe." He looked perplexed and scratched his head. "I just don't get it. They are great people. That's why I have them on the team, but they're both way behind in their annual sales objectives. It's already six months into the fiscal year."

Referring to the model in Figure 1 on page 8, Jed asked, "What is the distance between their current performance level and the results that they are committed to achieving?"

Graham thought a moment and then said, "To meet their quota, they would each need roughly two million pounds to close the gap."

"Yes, I see, Graham. That's their quota. What have they promised to you that they would produce?"

This question puzzled Graham. Jed could see it on his face. "Okay, coach, what precisely do you mean by 'promise'?"

"Let me put it this way: What has each player said to you that he or she would achieve? Or to what specific performance result have the players given you their word to hit this year?"

Graham leaned back in his chair and twisted a fountain pen. "We haven't really had that conversation. You see, our company gives every regional sales manager an annual sales quota. Now that you mention it, the teams had been complaining that their quotas were a bit lofty when they were published in January. You know, I really don't know what these two players are committed to accomplishing this year. For that matter, I don't really know what other players are committed to either."

That was a classic Thunderbolt!

Corky Spears attended a CoachLab in San Jose and stopped us after we finished the workshop. "I must tell you that this information will be valuable in my business. I hope what I'm going to say doesn't seem like diminishing your information, but I need to apply it to my teenagers. This summer the oldest wants to go to tennis camp and the other to a surf camp. We've talked about it and they're excited. The programs are excellent but expensive. To make this happen, it would mean we'd have to do without some extras. I must find out what they're willing to do to make the camps happen."

"Great. What do you think they might be willing to do?" Germaine asked.

Corky responded, "They could help around the house, say, doing things we pay others to do. Maybe even get part-time jobs." Then suddenly Corky smiled excitedly. "They can pledge half of their allowance each week for a camp fund and take turns cooking and doing yard work. This is a Thunderbolt! isn't it?"

Here's another Thunderbolt! You cannot coach players into achieving something that they aren't committed to achieving.

The Thunderbolt! level is coaching which produces results beyond the ordinary. It's that "palm-slapped-to-the-forehead" event. At the Thunderbolt! level, the player has entered ground that he or she once thought impossible. It's the level of wildly successful dreams.

Bless those who challenge us to grow, to stretch, to move beyond the knowable, to come back home to our elemental and essential nature. Bless those who challenge us for they remind us of doors we have closed and doors we have yet to open. They are Big Medicine Teachers for us.
—Navajo saying

Coaching the Dialogue

As a coach, you coach the dialogue in the pathway to the player's intended results.

You may want to say that out loud. The above sentence is that important.

But what does this mean?

It means that the coach places herself or himself in the future, in the intended results. Whenever the coach has a coaching session with the player, the coach listens for the obstacles that stop the player from reaching the intended results. The coach's job is to work with the player to clear those obstacles so the player can get or stay in action and move toward accomplishing goals. The objective of the coach is to have the player get to a place of choice, to have complete freedom in choosing the next move or be freed up to act.

I finally understood that to keep moving forward you not only have to look to the future, you have to inhabit the future.
—George Rodrigue, Louisiana Artist
(famous for the "Blue Dog" paintings)

In any coaching dialogue, first ask your player(s) for permission to coach before you attempt to do any coaching. Do this at each and every coaching occasion. Simply ask, "May I coach you?" This shifts the way your player listens.

At each coaching session, you, as the coach, facilitate the dialogue. Although the Greek root of the word dialogue is *di*, meaning two, the word dialogue is commonly used to describe conversational interactions among people in a group, such as a team.

This dialogue will actually make a difference for the player in terms of enhancing his or her ability to produce better results. We define a coaching dialogue that could make a difference this way:

> **coach-ing di-a-logue:** a conversational inquiry into any subject relevant to closing the distance between the player's current results and the intended results.

Current results could include the player's current situation, circumstances, environment or state of being. The coach/player dialogue can occur between player and coach or between a coach and team members.

Effective coaching dialogues always direct the conversation toward closing the distance between the player's present level of results and the intended outcomes.

Also, be cognizant of using these words or expressions: must, should, need to, and have to, in a command and control fashion. We try to avoid using these words and phrases as much as possible because they negate the spirit of coaching. Sometimes, however, they are appropriate, and we recommend using them in a non-directive style.

You coach the dialogue in the pathway to the player's intended outcomes.

"Coaching enabled our joint union/management team to resolve a backlog of nearly three hundred grievances in less than three months," said Mike Anderson, vice president of his local union in Ohio. "Normally, we carried years of baggage into our meetings. Our coaches got us to stow it outside the room."

This is a great time to coach the process or dialogue by asking questions. We recommend asking open-ended questions. This technique (or tool, if you prefer) allows the player to communicate freely about what's on his or her mind. (See Chapter 11 on "Questions Coaches Ask.")

We've found that this tool often allows a player to communicate in a way that is freeing. Have you ever experienced being able to just communicate what's going on with you and all of a sudden you feel like a load was lifted from your shoulders? We have.

Jed was once coaching the team leader of a special marketing team for a Fortune 500 company based in New Jersey. The team had been at work for about one month of a nine–month project.

Susan Centers, the team leader, said, "Jed, I just have to communicate something. Sorry, but I don't believe we can meet the targets that the executive team has set for us. I think the goals are a pipe dream!" Susan went on to tell Jed all the reasons that they couldn't achieve the team's chartered objectives. She described all the circumstances that would likely thwart them. For about twenty minutes, Susan poured out what was on her mind. She was articulate and adamant.

Jed just listened. Gradually, Susan's mood began to shift. Jed continued to listen.

Susan began to speak about ideas she had on dealing with the obstacles, possible ways to alter the circumstances. She spoke in this new, positive vein for about ten more minutes and then finally said, "You know, Jed, I think we just might be able to pull this one off. I feel so much better. You have been really, extra helpful today. Thanks a bundle, Coach! I'm grateful we had this time together."

Because you've read both sides of this coaching situation, you already know the punch line: All Jed had done was to listen. There may be times when that's your only role as a coach.

> *In the presence of the question, the mind thinks again.*
> —Nancy Kline, *Time to Think*

Ah, Those Busy Bees—
Action Versus Activity Model

The words "action" and "activity" are commonly thought to be different words used to describe the same phenomenon. They are often used interchangeably in ordinary conversation.

Actually, action and activity are poles apart. Once you recognize their distinction, you may have a Thunderbolt! It's been an enlightening experience for hundreds of people with whom we have worked.

Let's look at the Webster's Dictionary definitions and synonyms for these words that apply directly to our productivity.

ac-tiv-ity: 1. The quality or state of being active. 2. Energetic movement. 3. Natural or normal function. 4. A pursuit in which a person is active. 5. A state of motion. Synonyms: exercise, motion, functioning, operating, busy.

ac-tion: 1. The bringing about of an alteration. 2. A manner or method of performing an act of will. 3. Behavior producing a result or outcome. 4. A physical change, as in position mass, or energy. 5. A manifestation of intention. Synonyms: achievement, deed, performance.

See the confusion when these words are applied to productivity?

Note the word activity does not, by definition, suggest or even imply results or outcomes. Activity is described as a "state of motion," "functioning" and being "busy." Action is described specifically as "the bringing about of an alteration," an "achievement" or "deed."

Furthermore, action connotes "performing an act of will." We intentionally take action. You may be wondering to yourself, so, what's the point, and how does this apply to my coaching work? To my clients? To my students or my kids?

Look at the Action vs. Activity model in Figure 2, using the definitions:

The top half of the model is a bias for activity. Generally, people invest little time imagining or inventing the future or focusing on the intended results. Their attention is placed on identifying their immediate problems. They invest by far the greatest amount of time working on solutions to those "in-their-face" problems. This results in a future driven by activity or reactivity. It is, in a most profound sense, a bias for activity.

Oftentimes, players are mesmerized by activity. Have you ever had a colleague who never seems to stop sorting papers, filing forms, making

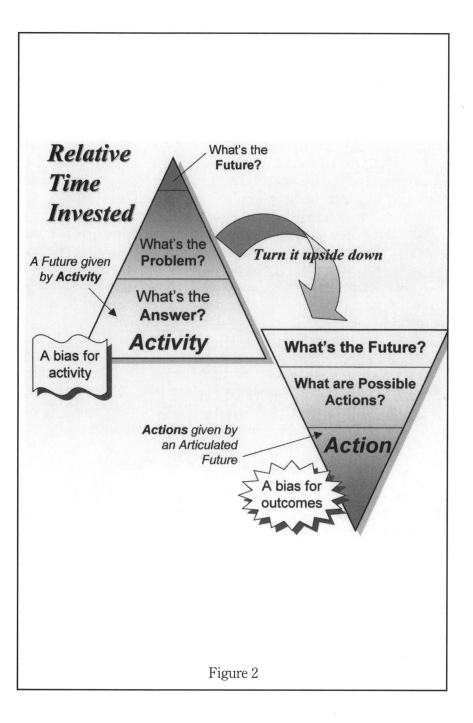

Figure 2

phone calls, replying to e-mail, or being connected to the Internet? The activity is hypnotic. You may have even thought, until you knew better, "Wow, lots of work is being done in that office." Activity like this creates the illusion that something is being accomplished.

Now look at the bottom half of the model and you'll see a bias for outcomes. If a player wants to reach the future or intended results, it is critical that he or she develops a bias for outcomes and a bias toward actions correlated to those outcomes. Once a player envisions the desired intended outcomes, then the possible actions the player may take to accomplish the results will begin to "bubble up" automatically. The intended results or future naturally begins to shape thoughts and actions.

As a coach, you must distinguish activity from action to assist your player in talking about where the actions and motivation come from. Action is related to some high value outcome, and activity isn't. In his book, *The 80/20 Principle*, Richard Koch explains Pareto's rule that 80 percent of your productivity comes from 20 percent of your actions. If you want to coach your player to accomplish the intended results, have the player shift to a bias for outcomes.

The key, then, is action. It's not words, it's action. It's not promises, it's results. It's not what you know, it's what you do. So accept absolute responsibility, and then, act, persistently.
—quoted by Anthony Falsone, author unknown

Merging the Two Models

We've just given you two models to add to your coaching toolkit. Philosophically, the models may sound okay. Now let's make them practical. Earlier, we talked about coaching the dialogue. You see, part of the dialogue is the player speaking about all the things he or she is doing. The player needs to talk about the activity that may be consuming time and, thus, disabling any movement toward the intended results.

One way to confront a player with this activity principle is to ask, "Sounds like you've been very busy. What results have you accomplished toward your ultimate objective?"

As a coach, listen to the player from the position of a bias for outcomes.

From that position, it will become clear whether the player is dwelling in the busy-ness of activity or if the player is in action and producing results.

Don't keep these theories and practical tools a secret. Share both models with your players to enhance their knowledge of how you listen to and work with them.

When one door closes, another opens, but we often look
so long and so regretfully upon the closed door that
we do not see the one which has opened for us.
—Alexander Graham Bell

Summary

In the previous pages, we've reviewed two models: the Go the Distance! coaching model and the Action vs. Activity model, both of which illustrate being focused on accomplishing results.

The Go the Distance! model displays the different levels of accomplishment and measurement, and introduces the notion that a coach coaches the dialogue in the pathway to the intended results.

The Action vs. Activity model will help you understand and discuss with your player that action is related to high-value outcome, and activity isn't.

In the next chapter, we'll pull out a new tool. It's the Coaching RoadMap and may be a road map to your success. We'll also cover the coaching contract for business and personal use, ways to assist players in setting appropriate objectives, provide an eight-point checklist which gives players the highest probability of achieving goals, and suggest five questions that will help players design pathways forward.

CHAPTER 3

You have freedom when you're easy in your harness.
—Robert Frost

COACHING ROADMAP – YOUR ROAD TO SUCCESS

Outcomes of this chapter:
- Discover the seven critical steps of the Coaching RoadMap.
- Learn the ten key points to include in any coaching contract.
- Find out how to assist players in setting appropriate objectives and how to help them win.
- Acquire an eight–point checklist necessary to design objectives, which gives players the highest probability of achieving them.
- Learn how to maximize your coaching effectiveness with e-mail.
- Learn five questions proven to help players design pathways forward to achieve their goals.
- Grasp the concept of feedforward.

It's true. The road to coaching success depends on having a good map and knowing how to read it. You'll want to add this new tool to your toolkit straightaway.

The Coaching RoadMap is an easy-to-follow, step-by-step process for coaching. The first words for each of the seven major sections of this process spell the handy acronym ROADMAP. (See Exhibit A.)

The Coaching RoadMap is a building process, beginning with the player/coach relationship and ending with the achievement of the player's objectives. Let's examine each section of the RoadMap pyramid, from bottom to top, beginning with the foundation, which is "relationship."

Let's start at the foundation of the pyramid, or list, and work up. If you've heard the adage, "It's all about relationships," then you know that this is crucial in coaching. The relationship must be there whether your

Exhibit A

The Coaching RoadMap

Performance (results)

Action/Dialogue
•Actions taken •What got done and didn't? •What's next?

Milestones
•Meeting intended objectives and promises regularly
•Completing the contract/making a new contract

Dialogue
•Permission •Conversations directed to closing the
distance between the present level of results and intended
outcomes •What would Thunderbolt! be for the player?

Action from the future
•Actions designed to correlate with an articulated future
•Absence of activity •The 80/20 principle

Outcomes contract
•Ground rules •Measurable targets/outcomes
•Timeframes •Expectations (yours/theirs)

Relationship
•Build credibility (bio) and rapport •Share philosophy

Figure 3

player is a Fortune 500 executive or a troop of scouts going out to sell cookies.

1. Relationship – ROADMAP
Build Credibility(Bio) and Rapport • Share Philosophy

Relationship is the foundation for your coaching work. This is true throughout the term of your coaching engagement. The purpose of the initial coaching session with a player is to build a relationship. How do you do that? Establish rapport and credibility as a coach.

Rapport can be built through a variety of means. To begin with, building rapport usually includes the sharing of personal backgrounds and each other's values. Shared values perform an extremely important function in the coach/player relationship. Shared values are a key ingredient in building trust in any relationship. The rapport becomes stronger over time.

The presence of trust is essential to effective coaching. If you find your closely held values don't match with your player's, you may want to discontinue the coach/player arrangement. In our experience, this has rarely happened. However, there have been a couple of instances where we have had to withdraw our offer for coaching due to a values mismatch. It's better for all concerned to discover this early on.

> *If you don't stand for something, you'll fall for anything.*
> —John R. Wooden, former UCLA basketball coach,
> winner of ten NCAA championships

Your coaching biography adds to your credibility. Just having one makes a statement: You are serious about coaching. Refer to our examples in Chapter 8 and then build your own.

Once again, throughout the term of your coaching relationship with a player, pay particular attention to the care and feeding of your relationship. It is the foundation for everything else that will and can happen.

"I'd been a business coach for a short time when my church group asked me to coach them through a building project for a new recreation center," said Luis Jones, who we met in Chicago last winter. "Before I said yes, I stepped back. Failure would not be an option on this coaching assignment. I determined that while I knew all these wonderful people personally, to get the best from my coaching skills, I needed to treat each with the same respect and assertiveness as I did with the clients who came into my business life."

Luis formatted dates for a series of meetings, met with the volunteers in a group, individually discussed goals, and helped them to make a plan. "I shared my coaching philosophy and bio; the players knew right off that this was a serious relationship. At each session, we immediately tackled the issues that would lead to success. Had I not done this, I have a feeling it would have turned into a 'Luis is too pushy' session."

If a man knows not what harbor he seeks, any wind is the right wind.
—Seneca

2. Outcomes Contract - ROADMAP
Ground rules • Measurable targets/outcomes.
Timeframes • Expectations (yours/theirs)

The outcomes contract is essential for effective coaching, a blueprint for success.

Prepare a carefully thought-out, written contract. Sure, it's possible to have verbal outcomes contracts, but we don't recommend it. Just as the writing of this book has made us better coaches, when you go to write your outcomes contract, you will discover aspects and items of your coaching relationship that you should make explicit. Writing the contract will no doubt help you uncover things you'll establish with your player straightaway so the issues don't become stumbling blocks later.

For example, one of the items in the contract might be this: how you will work together. This section includes some ground rules such as where and how often you will meet. It might establish what should happen if one of you discovers that you cannot keep a coaching appointment.

The following are the ten items we would include in any coaching outcomes contract:

1. **Purpose of the coaching.** What reasons does the player have for wanting coaching?

2. Scope within which the coaching will take place. Will the coaching take place strictly within business boundaries, or will it extend into the player's health and relationships?

3. Measurable outcomes (results) to be produced by the player and by what specific dates they are to be accomplished. Are the milestones well distinguished? The milestones, or checkpoints, are crucial for accountability as your player monitors progress. By the way, help your player set achievable objectives. To do so, you'll need to know about his or her historical results and enough about the nature of his or her business to do this properly. (See Chapter 11, Questions Coaches Ask.) It's debilitating for coach or player to attempt to hit totally unrealistic targets. (See Exhibit C, the Futurability for Objectives eight-point checklist, page 30 and Figure 4 below, The Outcome Continuum.)

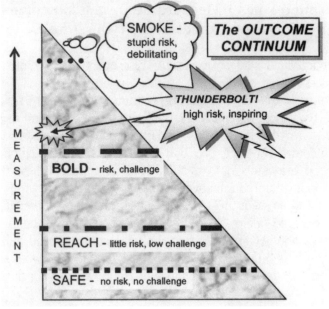

Figure 4.

4. Timeframe for the coaching engagement. State the beginning and ending dates of the coaching contract. This is usually six months to one year. Then, of course, you can renew the contract or write a new one.

5. **Cancellation clause.** This is typically a statement indicating that either party may cancel the contract for any reason in 30 days, after written notice.

6. **Ground rules.** Here are some examples: Ground rules include returning each other's telephone messages, voice mail messages within 24 hours, and e-mail messages within 48 hours. We promise open and honest communication with one another. We keep the sessions confidential; players need to know that whatever transpires in the sessions or dialogues goes no further.

7. **Financial arrangements.** How and when will the coach be paid? This is typically a monthly fee, or you may prefer to charge by the hour. You may want to include bonus opportunities based on the player's performance. How will expenses be handled? Who will pay for express mail, courier services, or long-distance phone charges for telephone coaching sessions or conference calls, for example? What about travel and accommodations? Will you charge for automobile mileage? Will you bill the client for travel time?

8. **Constraints.** What topics would your player consider to be "out of bounds" for you to discuss or for you to ask about?

9. **Expectations.** What are your player's expectations? What are your expectations?

10. **Coaching session frequency and format.** How often will you meet, and how long will your sessions last? Where will these coaching sessions take place? What percentage of the coaching sessions do you expect to be face-to-face and what percentage do you anticipate will be by telephone?

Exhibit B

Coaching Outcomes Contract for John P. Doe, Jr.

1. Purpose -
The purpose for the coaching is to:

(a) Obtain insights regarding clients and client situations.

(b) Expand the consulting/coaching practice.

(c) Learn and become proficient in the work redesign process for client companies.

(d) Be assisted in the writing of a "best selling" book, perhaps on Career Sales or Building an Independent Consulting Practice.

(e) Get organized for results, and stay focused on the "big picture," without dropping out the important details. Learn not to "over-commit" and take care of well-being.

(f) Master coaching by telephone and the coaching by telephone process.

2. Scope -

The scope of the coaching will generally be within the professional business arena.

3. Measurable Outcomes -

• Increase last year's coaching income by 30 percent and total revenues by 15 percent.

• Complete writing the first draft of a book by December 31.

• Have the book or its prospectus accepted by a publisher or agent by July 31.

• Bill for 80 days consulting/coaching by June 30.

• Experience having mastered telephone coaching by August 31.

4. Timeframes -

• The coaching engagement is intended to be at least one full year. This contract begins February 1 and ends January 31.

• This contract is renewable after January 31 by the agreement of both parties.

• The first six months of this contract includes a pay-for-performance aspect described in #7 below.

5. Cancellation Clause -

This contract may be canceled by either party, for any reason, with thirty days written notice.

6. Ground Rules -

• We will return each other's telephone messages and voice mail messages within 24 hours, and e-mail communications within 48 hours.

- We promise open and honest communication with one another.
- Confidentiality: Whatever we discuss will go no further than our conversations. This confidentiality includes our contractual arrangements and intended outcomes.

7. *Financial Arrangements* -

- John P. Doe, Jr. agrees to pay Jane Dough for coaching services the sum of $_____US per month, each month during the first six months of the contract period. These payments are due at the beginning of each month.
- At the end of the first six months, July 31, a $_____ bonus will also be payable to Jane Dough if John P. Doe, Jr. has:
  (a) Met his 6-month consulting objective of 80 billable days.
  (b) Had his book prospectus accepted by a publisher or agent.
  (c) Mastered telephone coaching skills and the telephone coaching process.
- It is anticipated that a new financial agreement and payment plan will be created by the end of the first 6-month period of the contract to apply to the second 6-month period.
- Long distance telephone expenses, travel, parking, and hotel accommodations will generally be paid for by the player/client, John P. Doe, Jr.

8. *Constraints* -

No topics have been declared to be "out of bounds" for discussion. However, it is anticipated that discussions will, for the most part, be centered around professional business concerns and the intended outcomes of this contract.

9. *Expectations* -

- John expects to be able to discuss his client engagements with Jane and receive coaching. He expects Jane to be a good sounding board. John expects to become a better consultant as a result of their coach/player relationship. John expects and appreciates spontaneous communications as well as scheduled coaching sessions.
- Jane expects John to be on time and prepared for each coaching session. She expects to learn from John and become a better coach and consultant as a result of their partnership. Jane expects her invoices for coaching to be paid in a timely manner.

---

10. Coaching Session Frequency & Format -
- Coaching sessions will be weekly, usually Tuesdays at 8:00 a.m central time, and will generally be conducted by telephone.
- Coaching sessions will ordinarily be one hour in duration. Should the need arise for substantially longer sessions, including face-to-face sessions, these can be arranged.

I hereby agree to the above terms and conditions and promise to fulfill each one.

_____   _____
Player: John P. Doe, Jr.   Date

_____   _____
Coach: Jane Dough   Date

To download a template of the Coaching Outcomes Contract, visit www.eaglesview.com.

These contracts vary widely, depending on the type of coaching involved as well as legal considerations. Please consult your attorney for the properly written contract for your state or jurisdiction.

We've been talking about coaching's business applications with some personal material sprinkled throughout. Now it's time to hear how parents have used their coaching tools in their home lives.

Madonna Smith, a long-time friend and a respected business leader in Texas, shared this with us: "I am a single parent, and during my entire parenting career, I truly dreaded Jonathan's teen years. These are the years when a child exits and a stranger takes over his or her body.

"Jonathan and I have always had an exceptional relationship. Then the teen years set in. We became separated. I said black, he said white. I am experienced in communication skills. I lead courses on my job. Taking it home is a totally different concept.

"Things began to happen at home, and I became increasingly disturbed by the people he hung out with and things he did. I decided to move to the coaching aspect. I became involved and took a stand for my son's life. At sixteen a contractual agreement seemed appropriate. I wanted his input. He said he was fine with whatever I did. A midnight conversation cleared the air on a number of issues and we signed the agreement.

"As parents, especially single parents, we need to help our children protect themselves and make good, mature choices. There are rules in all games we play, including rules for life. The contractual agreement is one way to make sure the rules of life are respected and kept intact. I feel this is an excellent ingredient in parenting. The young person is empowered in the right direction, with clear expectations and very clear consequences."

Here's the contract drawn up by Jonathan and his mother:

I, <u>Jonathan,</u> on this 31st day of <u>March,</u> do hereby agree to follow the terms of this Contract.

There are rules in life for a reason. One of the rules in our household is to follow the curfew both at home and legally. I must be in the house at 11:00 p.m. on weekdays and 12:00 a.m. on weekends. There will be times when I will run late due to complications or a late movie; when these times arise, I must call and let you know. If I am late and do not call for my tardiness, the consequence will be not to go out that weekend. If this happens on the weekend, then I cannot go out the next weekend. If it happens regularly, I cannot go out for two (2) weekends in a row.

I am 16 years old and should not be drinking/doing drugs. If caught with either, the license and car keys will be taken away from me. This will not be tolerated. Random drug testing will follow.

I must respect all of my elders. This includes my aunts and uncles, older cousins, teachers, and any adult in my presence. I must make time for my grandparents and respect them. I should not use profanity in their presence and if I do, I cannot use the phone for one (1) week.

Lying is simply something I must not do. If I do lie and it is a continuing bad habit, I will not be able to go out until further notice.

I agree with this contract:

_____

Jonathan Smith   Son

_____

Madonna Smith   Mom

There's always room for improvement, you know—
it's the biggest room in the house.
—Louise Heath Leber, Mother of the Year, 1961

Exhibit C

Futurability for Objectives Checklist

fu-tur-a-bil-i-ty: the ability of an objective to be realized in the future. Futurability has to do with the formulation and process in achieving an objective or outcome.

1. OWNED: Is this objective your own? Are you free from burden, guilt or sacrifice? Do you think you "should" or "have to?" Is it so significant that you'll be hampered?

2. RELEVANT: Will achieving this objective improve or forward your business or enhance profitability? Will it help fulfill one or more of your life goals? Is it worth doing? When imagining it completed, do you feel truly satisfied?

3. MEASURABLE: Is this objective able to be measured? Can you tell when it has been accomplished? Have you set a date when it will be done? Without a date to be achieved, it is not a realizable objective.

4. ACHIEVABLE: Do you have some sense you can achieve this objective, although you may not see precisely how yet? Or is it a hopeful fantasy or pipe dream?

5. INSPIRED: Are you challenged or inspired by this objective? Is it predictable, i.e. merely an extension of the past?

6. COMMITTED: Are you fully committed to the outcome, regardless of circumstances that may arise, or is this only a "wish" to be accomplished if things go your way?

7. SPOKEN: Is your objective in writing and part of your environment to call you to action? Have you communicated this objective to others? Have you made it public? Do you have the support of the key people in your environment?

8. COACHED: Do you have a coach, someone whom you are really willing to have be your coach for this objective? Will you be coachable?

3. Action from the Future - RO**A**DMAP
• Actions designed to correlate with an articulated future • Absence of activity • The 80/20 principle

At the beginning of a coaching relationship, and before you offer input, observe your player in action. Watch the player. Remember how Grandmother said, "Actions speak louder than words?" It's true with your players. Are they committed to the outcome? Need a clue? Look for an absence of activity.

Have the player apply Pareto's 80/20 rule to possible actions that they could take. As you remember, about 20 percent of the possible actions that could be taken will yield 80 percent of the final results that are wanted.

We call that 20 percent "high-leverage" or "high-value" actions. While it may not be exactly 80 percent and 20 percent, there will always be an imbalance between high-value actions and low-value activities.

On the 80/20 Rule: [Regarding] the doctrine of the vital few and the trivial many: there are only a few things that ever produce important results.
—Richard Koch, *The 80/20 Principle*

4. Dialogue – RO**A**DMAP
Permission • Conversations directed to closing the distance between the present level of results and intended outcomes • What would Thunderbolt! be for the player?

Have regularly scheduled coaching calls/meetings. This provides structure and certainty for the player.

Regular coaching sessions formalize the coaching process and provide impetus for the player to work to achieve his or her objectives. (See Chapter 9, the Coaching Call Plan Checklist, and the Coach's Value.)

Remember, in any coaching dialogue, first ask your player for permission to coach before you attempt to do any coaching. Do this at each and every coaching occasion. It's simple. Ask, "May I coach you?" As we said earlier, there's a shift in the way your player listens. This question means that a coaching dialogue is about to begin. You may ask permission several times in one session.

*Digging for gold is not the same as designing and building
a house. Analysis and judgment are not enough when
there is a need to design a way forward.*
—Edward DeBono, *Parallel Thinking*

The purpose of the coaching dialogue is "to design a way forward" from the player's present state to achieve the desired state.

We learned a long time ago that common dialogues don't move people forward in their commitments. Rather, common dialogues merely analyze, judge, and describe life. At best, they might be an exchange of information. All too often the information is an opinion rather than fact.

The coaching dialogue, on the other hand, is an extraordinary conversation. This dialogue seeks to design a way forward for the player to realize goals and objectives.

Here are five questions to ask your player during your dialogue. These questions close the distance between the player's current state and the desired state. (Refer to the Go the Distance! model in Chapter 2.) More often than not, these questions allow for new ideas and concepts to be generated. (For a more detailed description of the purpose and rationale behind each question, see Chapter 11, Questions Coaches Ask):

WHAT must happen? (What are the specific desired outcomes that must be achieved to close the distance between now and the next coaching session or during the next relevant timeframe?)

WHY do you think so? (Inquire whether the interim outcomes the player proposes are the appropriate outcomes to be completed at this time.)

HOW can that be accomplished? How else? How else? How else? (Yes, keep asking. Brainstorm possible actions to take to achieve the outcomes. Then select the best actions. New concepts and ideas may emerge.)

WHO will/should/could be the one(s) to do it? (Is there anyone else who could do these things? Delegation or contracting outside help may be appropriate.)

WHEN must this be accomplished? (Thinking from the future, by when should these interim outcomes be accomplished to be on track for achieving the ultimate objective?)

At each coaching session or dialogue acknowledge what your player's accomplishments have been since your last session. Acknowledge what was done as it applies to what the player said would be completed. Acknowledge what didn't get done as was planned.

Although by this time your player will have established the objectives that you are coaching to attain, it is important to find out what a Thunderbolt! result would be in this arena. You might ask, What would be a fabulous outcome for you? Remember, a Thunderbolt! is something entirely unpredictable and not promised, but highly desirable, something about which they dream. This information will give you insight into your player's psyche.

Record the player's next promised actions and promised results. Also record the things that you promised to your player.

5. Milestones - ROADMAP
- **Meeting intended objectives and promises regularly**
- **Completing the contract/making a new contract**

At predetermined dates, called milestones, check how the player is meeting the objectives. Is the player on track to meet the ultimate objectives? If the milestone happens to be the end of your coaching contract, acknowledge your player's accomplishments and celebrate! The celebration might call for a night out with the player, his or her spouse, and you.

Acknowledge what got done and what didn't get accomplished that was promised. Then design a way forward. Feedforward is the coaching term we use instead of the term feedback. Jerry Gauche, Vice President of National Oilwell in Houston, Texas, attended one of our courses. He uses feedforward to describe giving information (what we would normally call feedback) to someone to forward the player to the next level.

Stop for a moment and think about feedforward. It describes what coaches are doing. A coach enables someone to move forward. Feedback could merely be opinion, judgment, or evaluation without any intention of enabling the player to move ahead. Feedforward is intended to help us design a way forward.

A coach is someone who tells you what you don't want to hear, and has you see what you don't want to see, so you can be who you have always known you could be.
—Tom Landry, coach, Dallas Cowboys

You have another opportunity at this point, too. You can receive feed-forward on your skills as a coach. Ask your player for an evaluation on the coaching engagement. How was it? What worked and what didn't? Make notes of the feedforward for use in your next and other coaching assignments. You may complete/finish your coaching relationship with the player at this time. Or you may want to extend the contract or make a new one.

6. Action/Dialogue - ROADMAP
•Actions taken • What got done and what didn't?
•What's next?

Repeat steps 3 and 4.

7. Performance (results) - ROADMAP

Performance is the top of the pyramid. Results and accomplishments are why you are in the game. Each time a promised result is produced, find out what happened. What worked to accomplish it and what didn't work? Capture the "learnings," and if appropriate, do a little celebrating. Then repeat the RoadMap.

> *Dreams come a size too big so that you can grow into them.*
> —Jossie Bisset, author

Exhibit D
E-mail Checklist

Is this the best medium for your message? Does the receiver get e-mail messages regularly? Would this message be more effective if it were in a letter, sent as a fax, or provided by voice mail?

Plan your message so it can be as brief as possible.

Use subject section to indicate whether your message is Urgent,

---

For Your Information, a Request, a Promise, For Your Eyes Only or an Update.

Say up front what this e-mail is about, what topics, and how many.

Start with the bottom line. Then tell the "story," if necessary.

Avoid being cute.

Say whether you require a response and by when.

Your wildest dreams of robotics, miniaturization and the information superhighway will never replace people who are committed and accountable for making things work.
—Porché and Niederer

Summary

The Coaching RoadMap is a proven, step-by-step process that anyone can follow to deliver coaching. It is a building process beginning with the coach/player relationship and culminating with results. During the coaching engagement, the process is likely to be repeated many times. It depends on the nature of the player's objectives, the length of the coaching contract, and the frequency of coaching sessions.

Having a written Outcomes Contract with players is an essential step in the Coaching RoadMap.

Futurability (the ability of an objective to be realized) for objectives helps players and coaches thoughtfully design major objectives so that the achievement probability is higher.

Five simple questions open vast and creative opportunities for effective player action. To achieve a given objective, or part of an objective, (1) What must happen? (2) Why do you think so? (3) How can that be accomplished? (4) Who will/should/could be the one(s) to do it? (5) When must this be accomplished?

In our next chapter, we will give you tools to distinguish the roles of coaches and share the Coaching Scope, a model that embraces Thunderbolt! coaching.

CHAPTER 4

You cannot hope to build a better world without improving the individuals. To that end, each of us must work for his own improvement and at the same time, share a general responsibility for all humanity, our particular duty being to aid those to whom we think we can be most useful.
—Madam Marie Curie

THE COACHING SCOPE

Outcomes of this chapter:
- Learn a coaching tool to distinguish roles of a coach.
- Reinforce that coaching requires choices for the players.

Coaching is an invitation for a player to consider new perspectives. Like all skills, it requires practice and tools.

Our goal is to fill your coach's toolkit with information and models so that you can wrap your arms around this thing we call coaching.

The Coaching Scope model, which we'll give you in this chapter, has been shared with thousands of people. It's so important, we hope that you'll take time to review it. Think of the model as if it were the foundation of a house you're erecting. It must be sound and strong, especially if you plan to add a second story and create that incredible redwood deck above the patio.

In this chapter, too, we'll discuss how to make your foundation strong and sturdy along with tools, like mirroring, that will allow coaching jobs to become easier. Yes, once you understand these basics, you'll find that you'll be coaching in personal as well as professional relationships.

The Coaching Scope

The Coaching Scope is a modified version of the Range of Consultative Roles model, developed in the early 1970s by Marguiles and Raia.

Take a look at the model in Figure 5. As coaches ourselves, we'll first explain the model and then supply you with ways to use this coaching tool.

Figure 5.

The Coaching Scope is the landscape of consultative roles, from "content" orientation (being an expert), to "process" orientation (being a facilitator).

As you've noticed in the model, there are various roles that fall under the Expert or Content side. Consider the following examples:

- Technical Expert
- Trainer/Educator
- Problem Solver
- Tasks, "Pair of Hands"
- Resource
- Researcher (Data)
- Directive

What's common to each role? It is information and knowledge or skill. Each person requires a certain depth of knowledge in a particular area. You'd hire these people to give you the answer or solution to your problem. The key to this side of The Coaching Scope is having the answer.

Let's say your company is about to release a product that will be more innovative than pockets. You're sure to be interviewed on television and in the newspapers. We're talking big stuff. Why, there's even talk about a video and maybe a series of events to get the world to buy your product. So you hire Bertha, that exceptionally popular media consultant you've heard everyone raving about, to help you get ready for television appearances and those newspaper interviews. Bertha is an expert. She doesn't go on TV for you, doesn't stand in front of the camera or even whisper your lines; she coaches you before the big events so you know the process and can achieve the desired results. Bertha is an expert consultant telling you what you should do to be successful.

In the role of a "pair of hands," you may possess the knowledge or skill, but you employ someone to actually do the work for you so that you can invest your time and energy somewhere else. For instance, let's imagine you enjoy decorating, and your home is a showplace. However when your corporation moves into a new facility, you hire Cornelius, a specialist in corporate interior environmental design—he's dynamite. Besides, he magically gets the work done in half the time and makes it look like a million dollars. All that and he does it on a miniscule budget.

Now, let's look at the other side of the spectrum of The Coaching Scope with the Facilitator/Process. Some of the roles that occur on this side of the scope are as follows:

- Process Manager
- Objective Observer

- Inquiry, Questioning
- Mirror
- Feedforward (as discussed in Chapter 3)

What's different about the roles on this end of The Coaching Scope? Are you expecting the answer from someone in these roles? We think not. Rather, the expectation from people in these roles is concerned with the actual process or the direction in which something is going. More observation is taking place. Instead of giving the answer, the consultant or coach focuses on asking questions that will facilitate you in reaching the desired goals. When someone with these capacities is hired, the expectation is for the coach to observe us and to ask us questions to move us along.

> *You cannot teach a man anything.*
> *You can only help him discover within himself.*
> —Galileo

In coaching, the word "mirror" means that the person in the coaching role mirrors to us what we are saying. A mirror gives a reflection, that's all. Nothing is added to the image or reflection that you see, nothing except what you say, think, or interpret about your image. So it is with a coach who acts as an observer. You are given back verbally what you have said.

Can you imagine how invaluable that exercise can be? Many times in a coaching situation, when we repeat to the player exactly what he or she has said, the light goes on. The player knows exactly what should be done.

One of our clients/players, Bart Katz, a real estate developer from upstate New York, said recently, "What I really need to do is hire a CEO to run my company. However, the woman I want is not available for another two years."

Germaine mirrored back what Bart said: "I see. You really need to hire a CEO, and the person you'd like to have do that job is not available for another two years."

Bart responded, "That's silly, isn't it? If I really need a CEO, I'd better look for someone else." Thunderbolt!

In many situations, the players realize that their actions or words do not reflect what they are committed to. We often speak or act without thinking of the consequences. A coach who observes what we say or do points simple things out that can make a critical impact.

What About Coaching?

Take another look at the model in Figure 5 on page 38. The wavy section is how we depict coaching. In our coaching experience, we have observed that the main thrust of effective coaching falls in the middle. It's not solely content-oriented and not solely process-oriented. It's all over the map.

Sometimes a coach gives expert information, and other times a coach asks questions and observes the process. In many of the popular coaching programs taught, we've noted common disablements. For example, "Coaches should only ask questions and never give solutions or answers." These disablements are misconceptions or myths perpetrated by coaches and trainers of coaches who focus on certain approaches entirely too literally or who have made techniques rules instead of possible enabling approaches.

A Word About Advice

Should a coach give advice? Is advice the same as providing the solution or the answer? Here's Webster's definition of advice: (1) opinion given as to what to do or how to handle a situation; counsel. (2) (usually plural) information or report [diplomatic advice].

Now let's examine a key word in the definition for advice: opinion. The official Webster's Dictionary definition for opinion is: (1) a belief not based on absolute certainty or positive knowledge but on what seems true, valid or probably to one's own mind, a judgment; (2) the formal judgment of an expert on a matter in which advice is sought.

The caveat here is that, as a coach, advice should only be given to enable your player to reach an objective.

Too often coaches are geared to give their opinion or advice because they're trained to believe they should have all the answers. Beware. Doing so may jeopardize your effectiveness.

For those of you who are disagreeing with what we're saying because you've been trained to never give advice and only ask questions, you may be undermining your coaching ability.

One principle of coaching is to pay attention to your gut feelings. Yes, play your hunches. Allow your common sense and your intuition to inform you when you coach. To be effective, you support the player in achieving the objectives. That may include giving advice.

To realize this, start with the premise that people are experts in their particular profession. Your job is to assist them in forwarding their commitments and achieving their objectives. Therefore, when you share knowledge and information as a coach, you allow the player to make decisions. Your goal, however, is to allow the player to choose the information and knowledge that will give the player the means to achieve the goal. The important word here is "choose."

It's a common myth among some coaching theorists that a coach should never, under any circumstances, give their players solutions and answers to their players' problems or needs. These theorists believe that a coach should only empower a player by asking questions in order to help the player invent and develop his or her own answers and solutions.

Normally, we don't receive rousing cheers during our CoachLabs, but when we busted this myth during a seminar in Carmel, California, 30 people stood and clapped. Of course, we took time to bow. Seriously, the people, from executives to administrative assistants to professional coaches, had come to the seminar to learn how to become more effective coaches. They were delighted and relieved. Somehow, the majority of the men and women had been led to believe that a coach should only ask questions.

This news came as a Thunderbolt! Suddenly, they began to share times when they were asked to give answers to supply directions to players. They didn't. They held back because they were told that coaches were barred from doing so. Unfortunately, a dozen or so pointed out that they realized how one little answer or a nudge in the right direction would have greatly benefited their players. It would have saved time, frustration, and money.

After the ah-ha's and applause slowed, another question was posed: "As a coach, if I supply the answers or give a nudge, won't the player become dependent on me? Won't I be managing rather than coaching and leading?"

While it's true that providing answers and even supplying a nudge can speed a player to the solution and allow the player to succeed, it's important to note that you won't be disempowering a player. You only do that when you begin to manage the behaviors that are a result of the nudges. Further, you'll shortly learn how to utilize other coaching techniques so you need not depend totally on these basic tools.

Summary

The Coaching Scope is a model that vividly displays all the possible roles of a coach. The roles range from expert to facilitator with the wave of coaching moving everywhere along the spectrum.

We subscribe to the one that allows players to sort out for themselves what actions to take. If, as a coach, you possess expert knowledge that would forward players to achieve their objectives, we recommend that you share the knowledge with the players, giving options to make a personal decision. This is empowerment.

> *You cannot help men permanently by doing for them*
> *what they could and should do for themselves.*
> —Abraham Lincoln

We'll ask you to revisit The Coaching Scope later in the book. Take time to look at it and the roles coaches might provide. We believe you've got to invent coaching. Use the model, study it, and decide for yourself what your coaching profession is about.

Are you all over the scope in various roles or are you focused on one end of the scope?

Get ready to switch gears. Up to this point, we've talked about management and leadership contrasted with coaching; the Go the Distance! and the Coaching RoadMap models; and discussed The Coaching Scope. In the next chapter, you may be taken aback, baffled, and distraught. That's right. You're going to find out that you, yes, we mean you, are not "coach-able" and what you can do about the situation. We'll share tools to turn that resistance around and suggest methods that great players use to get the most from their coaches.

CHAPTER 5

Humans are wonderfully different and marvelously alike.
Human beings are more alike than unalike.
—Maya Angelou
Excerpt from a speech at Ohio Dominican College, December 9, 1993

RESISTANCE TO COACHING— THE I'S HAVE IT

Outcomes for this chapter:
- Discover why humans are not always agreeable to coaching.
- Learn how resistance can be turned around.
- Find out how great players use their coaches.

You're not naturally coachable. Further, to be coached and to coach, you may have to relearn some of the basic tenets of being a grown-up.

It's essential to know that you are not coachable, because if you're expected and determined to coach others, you must understand why you're not and why they aren't either.

Don't take it personally. We can see it in your I's. As adults we've been conditioned to be self-reliant, knowledgeable, independent, sovereign. It's the "I can do this myself" philosophy that makes us who we are today.

We spend a good measure of our lives trying to do everything on our own. But to coach and be coached effectively, we have to alter that thinking.

Start at the Beginning

When we take on the job of a coach, or we're asked to coach someone or a team, we start out, naturally, with most of the attention on ourselves. "What will I say?" "How will I say it?" "Will I be okay at it?" "Do I know enough?" "What should I do?" Then we jump in and start. However, amid all this self-concern, we fail to notice something essential. The player isn't listening.

Have you talked with a headstrong toddler lately? If the child is at the age when the favorite and sometimes only word is "No," you understand exactly what we mean. Regardless of what you may suggest, there's only one answer.

In a coaching situation, it's perfectly natural in the beginning to have players listening to what is in their heads and not to what the coach is saying.

Here are a few samples of what players may be saying to themselves while you are talking (and thinking that your player is listening):

- "Who are you to tell me..."

- "I should be coaching you because I know more about..."

- "I hope he/she can help me because I'm sinking fast."

- "So who died and made you king/queen?"

- "This stuff is just corporate babble that wastes my time."

- "My worries are over. I'll just follow this supposedly earth-shaking coach's advice, and if anything goes wrong, great day in the morning, I've found a scapegoat."

- "Ach, what a waste of time. I could better use the time to work rather than listen to this clown talk about coaching, a clown who has never done my job."

- "Holy smokes, when will the questions end? I thought I was going to get some answers from this so-called expert."

- "Who says I need a coach? I can do this myself."

Now, these are the business-related topics that might be circulating in your players' heads. If your players were brutally honest, any number of these things could be said within the first session. On the other hand, a player may be musing about non-business topics, such as which take-out place has the best Chinese cashew chicken, what stock to buy, or what to name a new goldfish. What about Spot? Or Fred?

You're getting the picture, right? Not pretty, is it?

It's sheer fantasy to believe that your player is always listening to you! Sure, you may think that the person is listening. He or she nods at appropriate times. The player smiles when you smile or tell a joke. But don't believe that there's true listening going on, even for a second. Why? Because we both know you don't always listen when others are speaking. So why would your player?

Chester Martin, an administrator for a large Washington State school district, attended one of our CoachLabs recently. When we began talking about this point, he mimicked the time-out sign for football and asked if he could share something. "This very thing happened earlier today," he began, and we could see he was still embarrassed. "I called the office to remind my assistant I'd be here at the seminar and to ask that he resolve a few issues that were on the fire. He wasn't there. He was out of the office at a seminar, too. When I got the receptionist on the phone, she was quick to point out that my assistant had reminded me of his seminar in front of her before we left the office last evening. I thought I was a good listener, but I'm going to have to work harder at it."

We all have chaotic minds. Like the administrator, we've all had the experience of "checking out," that is, pretending to be listening and not really doing so. Sometimes we're thinking of what already has been said. Other times we're planning what we're going to say as soon as the other person stops talking. Don't believe this? Ask your spouse, friends, or colleagues. Want the truth? Ask your kids. We all check out at times.

Right here and now, stop planning how you are going to coach and learn how to help your players listen so that they (and you) can profit from the coaching experience.

> *You gain strength, courage and confidence by every experience*
> *in which you really stop to look fear in the face.*
> *You must do the thing you think you cannot do.*
> —Eleanor Roosevelt

And Another Reason We're Uncoachable

In most western cultures, we have been trained to be independent.

Essentially, that means we're uncoachable. Almost from the second we're born, the adults in our lives teach us to do things for ourselves so that we become self-sufficient and require less help. "Oh, I'm so proud of you for picking up all your toys," your parent may have said.

By the time you entered kindergarten, you probably were doing your darnedest to be a grown-up. In schools, teachers tested our personal and individual knowledge on the subjects that were taught.

We knew we'd be punished for helping another student during a test. And if we got help from someone, it was called cheating. Were you ever allowed to take a team history, algebra, or Spanish test in school? Unthinkable. We were coached to do it ourselves. Again, it was the "I can do it myself" attitude.

With this mindset, many of us longed for the day when the lectures, training, and exams would be over so we could just do our jobs in our own way, at our own pace.

Teamwork has been a contradiction in American society clear back to Alexis de Tocqueville, that astute French observer who coined the phrase "habits of the heart" to describe our folkways. "Each man is forever thrown back on himself alone," wrote de Tocqueville in the 1830s, "and there is danger that he may be shut up in the solitude of his own heart." He called this tendency, lest you wonder where we got the word, "individualism." It is our great strength, the bedrock of the entrepreneurial spirit and innovation. Overused, it becomes our strongest weakness.
—Marvin R. Weisbord, *Productive Workplaces*

Did anyone say, What about team sports? Yes, we did have to learn to cooperate and coordinate with others to participate in team sports. For some of us, it was then we learned to receive coaching, too.

Who among us, even in elementary school, didn't have the thought once in a while that we knew better than the coach?

Further, in sports, there is a first and second string (big schools have third and even fourth strings). There are "starters" and the "backups." You started based on individual performance. But didn't you have to be a team player, too? Yes, you as an individual had to personally demonstrate that you could be a team player. Ultimately, the educational and athletic systems all pulled or pushed for individual achievement and accomplishment.

Certainly, we do not intend to mitigate or deprecate honors such as Most Valuable Player or Team Captain or All-City Champion. We believe strongly in personal recognition. Our point is to illustrate that most of us come from a culture of individualism, as de Tocqueville observed and Weisbord reminded us.

Not too long ago at an eastern high-tech Fortune 500 firm, we were training an eight-person executive team in coaching. We asked each of the executives to look into their lives to see if they could recall experiences that evidenced their own uncoachability. Slowly, each person shared personal experiences with each other. Then Jed asked, "Would you be willing to tell the group about these times of resistance to being coached?"

Coaching equals tools for self-knowledge versus prescription.
—Richard Barrett

Pat Freeman, one of the executives who helped organize the sessions, was the first to volunteer: "I am a little embarrassed to admit to this, and frankly somewhat ashamed." You can imagine that all heads turned his way. He shared that many years ago, and shortly after he had earned his Ph.D., he had written a technical paper that had been published in one of his industry's most respected scientific magazines. He had received numerous accolades from his colleagues, took the offered promotion, and became somewhat of a celebrity in his field.

"I got the idea for the revolutionary concept that I wrote about from one of my professors at M.I.T. I remember the exact day the concept was discussed. Heck, I'll never forget it." He said in all these years, this was the first time he had ever told anyone that his lauded paper had been inspired by this professor. He didn't want anyone to know that he had help. He said that the culture of his particular scientific arena only celebrated people who did original work and who did the work solely by themselves.

Pat needed to let people think that he had done it all by himself. The name of the game was "take all the credit you can get." Personally. Like most of us, he'd been raised to be independent and self-reliant and shaped by a scientific society. Getting help was not a sign of scientific prowess. Until that moment in our executive session, he had never given any credit to the person who inspired the original idea in him.

EXERCISE:

Where in your life can you see evidence that you were not coachable? Was it a time when you didn't or couldn't listen to a coach? Was it a time when you thought you had to do it all on your own? Take a few moments to inquire into your memory for events or instances of your being uncoachable.

Use the space below for any notes you might want to make:

_____

_____

_____

_____

_____

_____

_____

_____

Consider for a moment that you have been trained by your environment to be uncoachable. You might say that as human beings we are hard-wired to be that way. While we're not normally coachable, there are brief moments when we are coachable.

Here's an analogy:

Imagine a round, glass fishbowl about 12 inches high. Now envision that the bowl is filled with water with about an inch of sand settled at the bottom. What if you put a long stick into the bowl and vigorously stir the water? See the sand? It's swirling around up into the water.

Now, if you stop mixing it, the sand settles back down to the bottom, doesn't it? Human beings are a lot like the sand. From time to time, we're stirred up and become coachable, then we return to our solitary-thinking mode just as the sand settles back to the bottom of the bowl. That is, we once again become uncoachable.

How can you create an environment so that your players listen and can be coached?

How do you "stir up" a player's coachability?

It starts with the player's relationship to the objectives and then with the relationship with you. It turns out that the relationship with you and your coaching will almost always dramatically improve when the player has an appropriate relationship to the objectives.

Simply put: If the player deems the objective is worth achieving, and the more committed the player is to accomplishing it, the better he or she will listen. Therefore, the more coachable the player will be.

Conversely, if the player has no urgency, gives up, has no sufficient reward, and/or has no commitment to the accomplishment, the player will find it hard to listen to any coaching.

You cannot coach a player to achieve something that he or she isn't committed to achieving.

> *If a person imagines that she or he is either The Wild Man*
> *(know-it-all) or a Victim Child, the adoption of a mentor*
> *(or coach) is out of the question.*
> —Robert Bly, *Iron John*

The Weather Outside Is Frightful or The "Snow Job"

When players spend their coaching session doing nothing but trying to look good for the coach, the players are also uncoachable.

We believe that everyone can be coached, yet when the snow job occurs, everyone's time is being wasted.

How can you, as a coach, or part of the team that's being coached, spot a snow job? Just look around at your players and see those who think they don't need your coaching. They're right, in a sense. They don't need it because they can't use it competently. They think needing or utilizing coaching will make them look bad. What they want is to be proficient. Who needs something that they don't want and for which they don't have room? Their attention is on impressing, or snowing, you.

Life has trained us, at times, to look good in order to succeed. When the snow job is happening, the player may mean well because he or she wants to succeed with you, too! Therefore, the player cannot admit to you that there are any problems, any flaws or shortcomings.

When the player becomes the know-it-all, the be-it-all, there is no opening for the coach to contribute to this player.

> *Maturity would be doing something that would be good*
> *for you even if your parents suggested it.*
> —Author Unknown

Players exhibit the most coachability when they are willing to be candid enough with their coaches so that the players' weaknesses or blind spots may be exposed. It's then that the coach can go to work. He or she can contribute.

As a coach, look for ways during the coaching dialogue to provide openings to establish trust and an environment where listening can occur. That means, of course, that the coach must listen, too. We aren't saying that you, the coach, must be the one to do all the providing. No, the coach just creates the opening for whatever is missing. The source of the provision is preferably the player. That's when the player really wins! And they usually look good doing it.

How to Dis-empower a Coach

Samuel Johnson said, "Criticism is a study by which men grow important and formidable at very small expense." You may want to review the following critical tactics, just so you're aware of what could happen—so that you are not daunted by them.

Players who are uncoachable may attempt to find fault with coaches. Why? Because of that independent, self-reliant behavior. While it doesn't make sense to us, there are some people who can't ever allow others to be great, a hero, or someone of importance.

Sheryl Fletcher, a human resources administrator for a health care system in Arizona, has a quick sense of humor and genuinely enjoys coaching. She was part of a series of CoachLabs one summer. When we talked about this topic, she said, "I know just what you mean. In my family, anyone who excelled automatically got a big head. Heaven forbid, you never want that. In actuality, this thinking negates success. And furthermore, it makes it darn hard to fit through a door!"

Some people you'll meet as you coach must find "the flaw," something to bring the hero down to their level. They cannot allow people to be great. When the flaw is found, it somehow relieves them of any responsibility to learn from this accomplished person.

> *The weaknesses of great men and women*
> *are the consolation of fools.*
> —Don Marquis, Archie & Mehitabel

In our coaching experience, some players do this to nullify the coach's impact. It's quite simple. Don't like what the coach has to say? Find a flaw, anything will do, and in this player's mindset, the listening can stop. The flaw need not have anything to do with coaching or the reason why the coach has been hired. Rather, the flaw can be how the coach parks his or her car, or because the coach mentions the destination of a recent vacation or talks about going to a movie last night. Sound petty and off the mark? No, we're not kidding; this does happen. According to this game, when the player finds the flaw, he or she is home free. The player no longer listens. The coach is flawed.

You may be asking, "Surely there are smart players who let their coaches help them. What do they do to make themselves coachable?" We're delighted you've asked.

We Use 'Em and Never Lose 'Em— How Great Players Make Effective Use of Their Coaches

The great news is that some of the players you'll meet will embrace their own uncoachability. They intuitively manage it so that, as their coach, you can contribute to their success. Here are ten ways smart players do it:

10 Ways to Get the Most from Your Coach:

1. Choose this coach to be your coach. (Coaching doesn't work otherwise).
2. Reread the coaching contract (in Chapter 3) before each coaching session, until you "become the contract."
3. Be certain of your goals and objectives.
4. Be open to your coach's questions, observations, and suggestions; i.e., (a) make yourself coachable, open to take coaching, and (b) see yourself as a novice, strive to have a beginner's mind.
5. Communicate freely and candidly. To do this you must (a) err on the side of over-communicating; (b) not be afraid to be contentious with your coach. Constructive contention breeds creativity. Just be

sure it isn't your uncoachability doing the talking; and (c) keep talking until you experience that your coach hears and understands you.

6. Tell the truth.
7. Do what you say you'll do, when you say you'll do it. Keep your word and contract agreements.
8. Use your coach as a resource, not the answer.
9. Come to each coaching session prepared to (a) list the outcomes you intend to accomplish in this coaching session, and (b) do a fresh DreamMakers & DreamBrakers Audit before each coaching session. (See Chapter 13.)
10. Make it your job to inspire your coach. To do that, you'll have to be inspired yourself. At the end of each coaching session, tell your coach the things he or she did that made a real difference for you in achieving your objectives.

The will to win means nothing without the will to prepare.
—Henry David Thoreau

Summary

Some coaches live inside a myth that players always listen when the coach speaks. In fact, too many times, new players, or those who want to find a flaw with their coach, tune out help, conversation, and the chance to learn. Be aware of this factor as you coach.

Most of us come into business already steeped in the philosophy that we must be self-sufficient. Individualism is highly prized and doing things our way is somehow preferable, even if a coach's way works better.

Coaches are effective when it's recognized that just like themselves, their players are fundamentally uncoachable. Coaches become more effective when they listen to their players and are aware of the natural human resistance to being assisted or coached.

Players listen best when they are committed to producing an outcome that is beyond what they know how to do.

Next, we will share ways to increase player skills and build player confidence, give a new model for Thunderbolt! coaching, and reveal the four key player attributes.

CHAPTER 6

To be a star, you must light your own path and not be afraid of the darkness, for that is when stars shine brightest!
—Author unknown

THE COACHING SPECTRUM

Outcomes of this chapter:
- Be able to use a new model for effective coaching.
- Utilize the four key player attributes.
- Increase player skills and build player confidence.

In this chapter, you'll acquire a new coaching model to assist in designing effective coaching approaches, discover the four key player attributes and how to impact them to improve player results, learn ways to increase player skill and knowledge, and find out how to build player confidence.

You'll also be able to recognize "elf-confidence" and what to do about it, find out how to generate player motivation, uncover the five things that motivate players, and learn the five reasons players have for not taking action.

The Coaches are Watching
The Coaches are Watching

Good coaches constantly must gauge how much input to give to a player versus listening or asking questions. In The Coaching Scope model in Chapter 4, we talked about the variety of roles that coaches must play to be truly effective with their players. This ranged from a "content," or expert, orientation to a "process," or facilitator, mode.

How exactly does one determine which role to play or just how much input to give and what kind? Since a picture does supply a lot of words, take a look at Figure 6. It's The Coaching Spectrum.

The Coaching Spectrum incorporates The Coaching Scope with an added dimension. In this one, you'll find the player's range (his or her readiness to accomplish a particular task or objective).

We've taken The Coaching Scope and put it on end to create a vertical axis. Then we've made Player Range the horizontal axis. The Player Range has calibrated values 1 through 4. These ratings correspond to your assessment of your player's knowledge, skill, confidence, and motivation with regard to a specific task or objective.

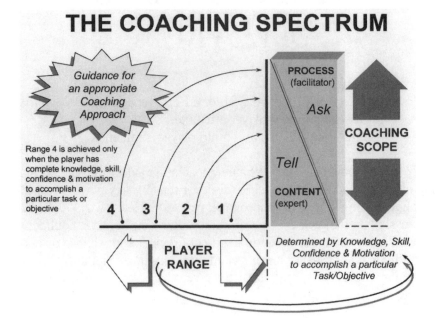

Figure 6 —The Coaching Spectrum
Co-created with Miguel Bernal, Ph.D. and Christopher Bernal, M.S.

Let's say you rate Chris, your player, at 4 on the Player Range axis. This would mean that in your estimation, Chris has complete knowledge, skill, confidence, and motivation to achieve the specific task or objective at hand.

A player you rate a 4 in Player Range requires little or no content, or input, from a coach. This is illustrated on The Coaching Spectrum by locating the number 4 on the Player Range axis and then following the curved arrow from the dot to the vertical axis on the right, The Coaching Scope. As you can see, The Coaching Scope indicates little content is required, and your approach or role as coach should be one of predominately facilitating, listening carefully and asking questions.

Now let's suppose that in your estimation, Terry, another player, has sufficient knowledge and motivation to achieve a particular objective; however, Terry needs help in the other two player attributes. That is, you believe this player lacks the skill necessary to achieve the objective. In your coaching sessions (other conversations and meetings, too), you hear a lack of confidence on Terry's part as well. Therefore, you would rate this player a 2.

For the sake of workability and simplicity, we assume each attribute to have equal weight and none is more important than another.

With Terry as your player, you'd work in a way that this player could acquire the skill necessary to achieve the objective, and do something to build the player's confidence.

Our premise is that if your player possesses sufficient knowledge, skill, confidence, and motivation to accomplish a particular objective, the odds of achieving it are quite high. While this might seem like common sense thinking to many of you, it could be a Thunderbolt! to some.

Knowledge, skill, confidence, and motivation are the four most critical attributes to consider about a player in relation to their desired outcomes.

Are there other things to take into account, such as time and resources available? Yes. However, these are circumstances outside the control of most players. They are not attributes of the player or person. Circumstances, other people, capital available, equipment, materials, the market, etc., all have to be taken into account when you consider The Coaching Scope and the Player's Range.

Let's look back at Terry, the player we invented for the previous example. It could be that Terry needs additional computer skills to be more effective. That's easy. We could recommend that Terry attend computer workshops to gain the skills. However, if the computer system Terry's company uses crashes often and is older than dirt, production is still not going to be achieved at the rate desired.

As a coach, you cannot directly do much about these things. What you do have direct access to is your player's attributes: degrees of knowledge, skill, confidence and motivation.

We cannot direct the wind...but we can adjust the sails.
—quoted by Charles Ulysses Porché, Sr., Author Unknown

Players require knowledge and skill to handle time, circumstance, and the physical universe. They need confidence in place of fear. And they must have adequate motivation or at least sufficient urgency to take any action at all toward the objectives. Throughout this chapter, we'll discuss how these four key attributes are related to one another.

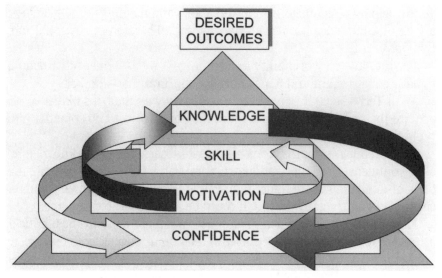

The Desired Outcomes are obtained as a function of the four key player attributes:
knowledge, skill, motivation and confidence:
the degree to which they are present and their inter-relatedness.
Some examples: 1. Acquiring *knowledge* and *skill* requires *motivation*.
2. Increases in *knowledge* and *skill* improve *confidence*.

Figure 7.

Let's look at Exhibit E on page 59 for a moment, please, at our definitions for the four Player Range areas. Being clear about the definitions for the key player attributes has proven to be extremely helpful in our coaching endeavors.

Most people unwittingly consider knowledge and skill to be the same thing, and we've seen this misinterpretation cause trouble. It's a myth. They are, in fact, very different and quite distinct.

Richard Pascale, author of *Managing on the Edge*, gave us a simple

Exhibit E

PLAYER RANGE
Definitions

(THE COACHING SPECTRUM)

• Knowledge
Having familiarity, awareness, understanding, or education. Within the range of one's information.

• Skill
Natural or acquired facility. Demonstrated ability to perform. Great proficiency.

• Motivation
Possessing sufficient inspiration, commitment, courage, incentive, or reason to act. A compelling basis for action or decision. Encouragement. Enough urgency to take action.

• Confidence
Firm belief in one's own abilities. Trust and faith in oneself or others. Self-reliance, self-assurance. A sense of self-sufficiency. Being or feeling certain.

simulation, which vividly demonstrates the difference between knowledge and skill, while we were co-leading a course with him in London.

Richard asked the participants if they knew how to write their name. We wish you could have seen the looks on the players' faces, and if we could read minds, we know we could have heard some mutter, "And we paid money for this?"

However, they all said they knew how to write their name, and then Richard said, "Okay, go ahead and write it now, but with the hand you don't normally use to write."

Again the group chuckled, and good-natured people all, they awkwardly wrote out their names as best they could with the unfamiliar hand. Richard said, "You see, just because you have knowledge about something doesn't mean you have skill in the same area. You all have the knowledge necessary to write your own name. But you have little skill in writing your name with your 'wrong hand'."

Clearly, having familiarity, awareness, or understanding with regard to a subject does not ensure that the player can perform with great proficiency or facility. Even though a player is confident that a particular result can be produced, it doesn't guarantee that this person is motivated to do so. (Note: You may have just had another Thunderbolt!.)

We've witnessed coaches make the assumption that a player will do something because the player has faith in his or her own ability to make that something happen, only to be surprised when the player doesn't do it. We've made this mistake ourselves.

Let's revisit Terry, our created example. Terry needs to learn computer skills. Terry is smart and friendly. Terry's a willing worker. But Terry's not motivated because the computers at the player's company are old, don't work well, and won't allow Terry to get anywhere close to achieving the corporate objectives.

Remember, action doesn't necessarily follow confidence. There are thousands of things that you are confident that you can do, aren't there? Yet, you aren't necessarily motivated to do them all, right? Jed is a pretty fair swimmer, yet he's not particularly motivated to swim the English Channel. Germaine likes cycling and toys with the idea of biking through Europe, but she isn't motivated to train for a serious competition like the Tour de France.

> *Sometimes you just have to take a leap, and build*
> *your wings on the way down.*
> —Kobi Yamada, author

Sometimes we find it useful to rate players in each of these four categories, on a scale of 1 to 10.

For example, on the Player Range, a player we'll call Jack would rate a 3 in motivation. That gives us some direction. Taking each category and rating him on a scale of 1 to 10, we assess that Jack is about an 8 in knowledge, a 7 in skill, a 10 in confidence, and a 3 in motivation. So, although it is clear he needs something to provide motivation primarily and immediately, we also know from the 1 to 10 scale that Jack might benefit from some skill building later on. Since we rate Jack a 10 in confidence, we shouldn't have to invest much in building his confidence.

This is our maxim: Spend little or no time teaching fish to swim.

We focus far more intellect and far more thought into what we do in practice than other teams do. We have five or six skills or techniques that we want to teach our players to be able to use in carrying out his assignment, where our opponents usually will have only one or two. Many other teams take a more simplistic approach. They teach their players one approach or technique. Our approach gives our players more dimension.
—Bill Walsh, while coach of the Stanford Cardinal football team

Never Fear, Help Is Here

How can you help players to improve their knowledge, skill, confidence and motivation? This is the core of coaching and unless you have some of these tools in your toolkit, you may as well hang it up.

It's one thing to diagnose a player's score in the four key attributes. It's quite another to help players improve in those areas. We have discovered myriad methods to do this, and we have listed them below for you.

Here's our proven list of ways to help players acquire the knowledge needed to perform certain tasks and accomplish particular objectives. We've left lines at the bottom for you to add ways that can help players to improve knowledge:

15 Ways to Improve Player Knowledge

1. Have your player read and study while baroque music plays in background.
2. Have your player listen to audiocassette tapes or CDs in the car or at home, on topics to improve knowledge.

3. Have your player watch videotapes.
4. Have your player research information on the Internet.
5. Have your player take courses to increase knowledge.
6. Ask your player what he or she is learning from a study program.
7. Give your player an exam; have others test him or her. Create a self-monitoring test for your player.
8. Have your player participate in accelerated learning games.
9. Have your player share what has been learned with others so that he or she can further master the material.
10. Have your player observe other people doing what he or she must do.
11. Have your player hang out with people who have expertise in the area.
12. Introduce your player to others who have successfully done what your player must accomplish.
13. Teach your player what he or she needs to know.
14. Have your player locate a mentor in the area.
15. Have your player hire or rent the knowledge needed.
16. _____
17. _____

Ideas are funny little things. They won't work unless you do.
—quoted by Esther Worrell Niederer, author unknown

How to Increase Skill

Here's a list of ways to increase your player's skills:

11 Ways to Increase Player Skill

1. Have your player practice.
2. Have your player participate in games that increase skill.
3. Create role-playing opportunities for your player to elevate his or her skill.
4. Have your player apply his or her knowledge at every opportunity. Invent opportunities to do so.
5. Have your player experiment with the skill; this can free him or her up.

6. Train your player, or have the player get a trainer.
7. Have your player learn 30 times more than he or she will ever apply.
8. Have your player play accelerated learning games.
9. Have your player compete with others to sharpen skills.
10. Have your player hire or rent the skill that's needed.
11. Ask your player to observe others demonstrating the skill.
12. _____
13. _____
14. _____

Confidence may well be the single most important of human attributes because confidence alone liberates people from inhibiting fears. Confidence is the quality that enables people to move forward in life and manage its turmoil. Without confidence, people flee from reality, continually seeking outside protection from things they must confront themselves.
—Judith Bardwick, *In Praise of Good Business*

Building Confidence

Improving the player's knowledge and skill can go a long way in building confidence. When someone knows more about a subject than they will ever have to use, it has the effect of reducing fear.

Also, as a coach, being confident and certain sometimes increases a player's confidence, as well.

When we say confidence, we mean genuine self-assurance that is partially based in knowledge and skill. As mentioned earlier, there is another kind of confidence, really a false confidence, that we whimsically call "elf-confidence," and it is the direct opposite of self-confidence.

Elf-confidence is sort of an arrogant and "airy-fairy" notion. It is an unfounded belief that you can handle it, in spite of your lack of knowledge and/or skill, or that somehow the magic elves will handle it for you.

For example, we were in Canada last year preparing to conduct a 40 participant reengineering training session for a building products company. One of the simulations or games that we planned to run was a daylong exercise that was quite complex.

It had hundreds of logistical parts to be managed. It was tricky but so effective. In addition, there were intricate rules that had to be followed by the participants, and, as the coaches, we needed to ensure everyone followed those rules for the simulation results to be valid. Sounded perfect and exciting and fun when we organized everything on the tables at our offices in Texas.

However (did you hear that however coming?), to make things interesting, we discovered the night before the event that the leader's guidebook hadn't arrived with the other materials that were shipped for the event. It was in Texas; we were in Toronto. It was nine at night.

Germaine and Carlin, a consultant provided by the client, were scheduled to be co-facilitating this simulation. Germaine and Jed had led this simulation a few times before, but not for a couple of years. The other consultant had never run nor seen the simulation.

Time was slipping away. We went through the material for the tenth time and realized the leader's guidebook definitely wasn't in all those FedEx boxes.

It was now 10:00 p.m. Before 8:00 a.m. tomorrow, we had to write some sort of leader's guide from memory, a timeline for the day, organize and set the room with a myriad of materials. While we were working, we noticed that Carlin, our new colleague, wasn't paying much attention to what we were attempting to explain to her. She didn't seem to grasp the enormity of what had to be done in order to be ready for the next morning.

In fact, she would frequently interrupt us saying enthusiastically, "Hey, don't worry about it, guys. We can handle this. No problem!"

> *It's not what you don't know that can hurt you*
> *but what you think you know and it just ain't so.*
> —Satchel Paige, possibly the greatest
> professional baseball pitcher of all time

After a while, it became obvious that our new colleague was suffering from a case of elf-confidence. She was in a fake-it-til-you-make-it mode. She lacked authentic self-confidence, grounded in knowledge or skill.

Germaine stopped the show and addressed the issue. She asked Carlin, "May I coach you?"

Carlin said, "Of course, you may." Thank goodness!

Germaine explained that without adequate preparation and practice, the simulation tomorrow would surely be a disaster for everyone. "Carlin, your effervescence is welcome. It's refreshing. I appreciate it. Yet, please direct it toward learning what you've got to cover tonight in order to be successful with and for the participants tomorrow. If you'll do that, we can all have some real confidence. And Carlin, I really need your help tomorrow."

Carlin got the message and she went to work in earnest. Happily, the next day the simulation worked brilliantly for the participants, and Carlin did a great job on her part. Had we not recognized the elf-confidence as quickly as we did, the result might have been quite different.

> *There is really nothing more to say—except why. But since why is difficult to handle, one must take refuge in how.*
> —Toni Morrison, *The Bluest Eyes*

As a coach, you must know how to build a player's confidence. Here are some tools to add to your toolkit. Feel free to add to this list from your experience:

13 Ways to Build Player Confidence

1. Be confident, have certainty about yourself and your convictions.
2. Earn your player's trust. Be a person of integrity.
3. Make things simple, doable.
4. Tell your player he or she is able, capable.
5. Tell your player he or she can do it.
6. Acknowledge your player for what he or she does that works.
7. Inspire your player to feel great about him/herself.
8. Tell your player inspiring stories and quotes.
9. Introduce your player to other clients who have successfully done what your player must accomplish.
10. Remind your player of similar accomplishments he or she has achieved.
11. Make sure your player has the tools and resources for the task.
12. Have your player get the right people for the job.
13. Utilize the DreamMakers & DreamBrakers Audit to give the player an eagle's view of their project. (See Chapter 13.)
14. _____
15. _____
16. _____

It sometimes seems that intense desire creates not only opportunities, but its own talents.
—Eric Hoffer

How to Generate Motivation

A person possessing an "intense desire" is motivated. That intense desire creates opportunities and perhaps even its own talents or skills. This is another reflection of the inescapable inter-relatedness that the four key attributes share.

Primarily, there are four things that motivate us:

1. Recognition
2. Challenge
3. Growth/Learning
4. Reward

Take a moment to consider a fifth—fear. We aren't recommending that you should use this motivator as a desirable external coaching tool. We have, however, observed (and experienced ourselves) that fear can be a powerful motivator for players. To disregard its power is to cut yourself off from part of your player's humanity.

Fear is something to take into account, something to be aware of. It can provide a positive urgency or energy, which can make fear highly productive. It can also stop people in their tracks, and inhibit any kind of fruitful action on their part.

We hope you will never be the one who instills the fear. There are so many more effective motivational tools. However—and remember this as you coach—you will need to know how to alleviate the fear when your player is frozen by it.

Let's say a child or teen isn't doing well in school. It could have nothing to do with learning, but rather be a fear of failure, fear of revealing a secret (such as not being able to do multiplication tables, especially the 9s), or of an imagined fear you may think too trivial even to mention (such as the crossing guard being an evil wizard). Keep in mind when dealing with fears—they're real to the people who have them.

Nelson Hoff, a vice president of facilities for a nationally known home improvement store, was in one of our CoachLabs. When we talked about fear, he just had to add his experience. "About ten years ago, corporate mentioned that things would be reorganized and wanted to know my plans for the future. First it was only talk. I knew that with the promotion, which I really wanted, I'd have to interact and communicate well with contractors, attorneys, and planning departments for cities all over the country. I've got the degrees to prove I'm qualified, but not a native English speaker. Sometimes I would find expressing myself to be a challenge. I got tongue-tied with small talk, too. I spent five months hoping for the promotion and that same time, dreading it. I was paralyzed with fear. Then one of the other vice presidents suggested I attend Toastmasters with her." Nelson said his colleague coached him through speeches, which he eventually gave, "and by the time corporate figured out the organizational plans, "I had so much confidence." As Nelson said, "The rest is history."

Since fear is a huge factor, though often not discussed by coaches, you must be aware of its presence. You just may need to do something to free up your player for him or her to take effective action.

> *People who feel unsafe lack motivation, tolerance,*
> *compassion, and the ability to innovate.*
> —Jennifer James, *Thinking in the Future Tense*

EXERCISE:

Forced Ranking Motivators

Time to flex your coaching muscles.

Try force-ranking the five motivators for yourself: Recognition, Challenge, Growth/Learning, Reward, and Fear.

Be honest. No one is looking. What motivates you most?

Puzzled? Recall specific times in your life when you've accomplished something great. What was your dominant motivation then? Was it reward? Was it recognition?

First, write down the motivator that influences you more than any other. Then, write down the one that influences you least. Rank the others in between. Use a pencil, as you may change your rankings during this exercise:

1. _____
2. _____
3. _____
4. _____
5. _____

You might ask your players to force-rank these five motivators. You may help them reveal their "hot button" (really a Thunderbolt!) and give you insight into how to coach each of these individuals.

Tentative efforts lead to tentative outcomes.
Therefore, give yourself fully to your endeavors.
—Epictetus, Greek teacher and philosopher, 55-135 A.D.

Teams can have motivators and share them, too. For example, we were coaching a work redesign team not too long ago. Representing a biotech firm based in Southern California, the team's task was to get rid of any needless bureaucracy they could find in their company. It was a challenge and we were glad to be part of the change.

The desired outcome was to free up the employees so they could do their jobs more easily and effectively. At the corporate level, the executives had challenged and authorized this team to eliminate all the archaic, useless and invalid policies that existed. They were asked to do it all within six months. From what we could see there were plenty of policies that needed work.

During the first three months, the team worked diligently to document all the company's policies. They identified a long list of policies that could/should be thrown out. But when it came time to drop the curtain on the ineffective policies, we observed the team dynamics. They were reluctant to take action.

Were they paralyzed with fear? What was holding them back? It was as if they were entirely unwilling to take any decisive action.

H. Ross Perot, when he was a board member for General Motors, said, "Revitalizing General Motors is like getting an elephant to tap dance. You find the sensitive spots and start poking."

By doing a little poking, that is by asking questions, we uncovered the reasons for not acting. They had convinced themselves they "must be careful and proceed slowly, with great caution."

Their concerns may seem valid if you've ever been in such a position.

They wondered: "What if we eliminate a policy that is actually needed? What if we just don't understand what a policy is for or meant to do? Let's say we eliminate it, and bad things happen? What then? We'll be food for the wolves!"

Collectively, they were stopped by the fear of making a mistake.

Meanwhile, Fred, the team's executive sponsor, had heard about the team's reluctance to act due to fear. In addition, the executive team had expected to see some policies eliminated by a certain date, and Fred was asked what was happening. Fred visited the team during one of their meetings and listened attentively to their worries and concerns.

After the team members felt they'd said it all, Fred folded his hands in front of him and said, "I understand your concerns. My view is simple, really. This is part of the risk we all have to learn to take to be an excellent company. You all know me. Here's what I suggest: The possible consequences of your not taking action are far worse than taking action and making mistakes. Please eliminate 30 of the useless policies on this list by next Friday. Otherwise, I'll be forced to find a team who will. Any questions?"

There were no questions. Thirty policies were eliminated by Friday. Same motivator, fear but a different outcome: urgency to take decisive action.

Again, we do not recommend that you use fear as a motivator, but you will find that it is present from time to time when coaching.

The sea is dangerous and its storms terrible, but these obstacles have never been sufficient reason to remain ashore.
—Ferdinand Magellan, 1520, captain of the first known sailing expedition to circumnavigate the globe.

Motivation is Really the Player's Job

Ultimately, the player must be responsible for his or her own motivation to perform at the highest level. In the interim, the coach may have to provide some motivation or show the player how to become motivated. Keep in mind that the following works in business and can help your volunteer group or civic organization, too.

Here is our list of ways to assist players with motivation:

11 Ways to Motivate Players

1. Tell your player inspirational stories or share inspirational quotes.
2. Have your player watch inspiring films.
3. Have your player invent a reason to act, that is, to find a compelling basis for taking action or making a decision.
4. Have the player invent urgency.
5. Invite the player's commitment.
6. Provide encouragement.
7. Acknowledge the player for every right move along the way.
8. Set up a game with little rewards in it for the player along the way.
9. Have the player announce his or her commitment to others whom the player respects and knows.
10. Have the player imagine vividly the inspiring future enjoyed as a result of accomplishing the objective.
11. _____
12. _____
13. _____

Some men (and women) have thousands of reasons why they cannot do what they want to, when all they need is one reason why they can.
—Willis R. Whitney

Hey, Who Put on the Brakes?
When Players Aren't Taking Action

Here are the top five reasons why players don't take action. You may want to share this with your players because we've found even players themselves need to know and understand why they're not motivated to move.

1. MONEY
   a. Player has no money available,
   b. or not enough money,
   c. or something is too expensive.

2. TIME

   a. Player has no time available,

   b. or not enough time,

   c. or something isn't worth the time investment required.

3. FEAR

   a. Player imagines unfavorable consequences from taking action,

   b. and player believes inaction to be less dangerous.

4. TRUST

   a. Player lacks trust or faith in the coach,

   b. or mistrusts the coach,

   c. or player lacks self-confidence or certainty.

5. URGENCY

   a. Player feels no urgency to act,

   b. or insufficient urgency to act,

   c. or the player experiences too much urgency, so much so that he or she is "frozen" and can't move (see FEAR above).

Summary

The Coaching Spectrum is a potent, analytical tool to help determine the best coaching approach with each player. It can take the mystery out of coaching and give ways to enhance your coaching ability.

The four key player attributes are knowledge, skill, confidence, and motivation. Armed with this information, you can be an effective coach and an exceptional asset to your players.

Five things motivate people: recognition, growth/learning, reward, challenge, and fear. The forced ranking of these can reveal the best coaching strategy.

When players don't take action on things they know they should, it is usually because of one of five things: no money, no time, fear, no trust, or a lack of urgency. Uncovering these can make short work of freeing players to take action and finding new ways to get the job done.

In the next chapter, you may have another Thunderbolt! We're going to address another essential aspect of coaching: effective listening and ways to engage your player.

CHAPTER 7

There was an old owl who lived in an oak,
The more he heard, the less he spoke;
The less he spoke, the more he heard,
O, if men were all like that wise bird!
                              —Punch, LXVIII, 155 [1875]

HOW COACHES LISTEN

Outcomes of this chapter:
   • Utilize innovative listening methods.
   • Know what coaches listen for.
   • Learn ways to engage the player.

Over the years, we've seen some men and women who have attended our CoachLabs discover that listening is a Thunderbolt! It happens as they realize that listening is one of the key ingredients of coaching. Somehow, they were previously told or taught that coaches did most of the talking.

Listen Up, Pal

It's our hope that you realize that listening may be the most important aspect of coaching. This chapter is written under the assumption that you have the ability to listen. Ponder this for a moment, won't you? Excellent coaches stop talking and allow players to speak.

The following quote eloquently describes how a powerful coach listens to his or her players:

Listening is a rare happening among human beings.
You cannot listen to the word another is speaking if you are pre-
occupied with your appearance or with impressing the other, or try-

73

ing to decide what you are going to say when the other stops talk-
ing, or debating about whether what is said is true or relevant or
agreeable.

Such matters have their place, but only after listening to the word
as the word is being uttered. Listening is a primitive art of love in
which a person gives himself to another's word, making himself
accessible and vulnerable to that word.

—William Stringfellow, philosopher

How many people do you know who listen the way Stringfellow describes?

When coaching, do you listen to every word, or are you thinking about the next thing that you will say?

In the moments when you know you are listening the way Stringfellow describes, what happens with the player? In our experience, the player communicates and expresses her/himself fully. Once the player realizes that he or she will have a chance to talk, something incredible happens. The player becomes assured that he or she will not be criticized. The player begins to partner with the coach with complete confidence.

If, as a coach, you have thoughts about what you should say next or concerns about how to impress your players, the attention is going in the wrong direction. It's on you. When this happens, it's a sure bet you're not listening completely to the player. You will probably misconstrue something that the player is telling you or the topic under discussion.

When the attention is on yourself rather than the player, all sorts of thoughts come into play: Am I saying the right thing? What if he or she finds out that I'm really not smart? What if the player asks something I know very little about or nothing?

Thunderbolt! If you're all wrapped up in your own thoughts, your message becomes a tangled web to your player.

In previous chapters, we talked about coaching the dialogue in the pathway to the player's intended results. Listening is the highway on which the dialogue "drives." It plays a critical role here. For you, the coach, to be fully available to the player, begin with yourself. You have to put aside obstacles that keep you from being the best coach you can possibly be for this player. Any concerns, fears, or anxieties you may have about yourself or the player, influence how you listen and coach.

"Not me!" you may be saying, especially if you are a seasoned coach, have been coaching for years, and have been successful. We invite you to consider that overconfidence and sureness can have you listening ineffectively, as well. You, too, may misconstrue what someone is saying.

The danger with coaching lies in the perceived need for the coach to appear brilliant, to seem to have all the answers. When coaches are focused on looking wonderfully clever, they do not listen long enough. They summarize and interpret and direct far too early in the session.
—Tina Breene, executive coach,
as quoted in *Time to Think* by Nancy Kline

The following are a few questions and points to consider, which could influence how you listen to your players. Read through the ideas and see if any spark further investigation. There are no right answers, but answer honestly.

- Are you new at coaching and concerned whether you can make a difference with your player?
- Do you know your player's business? If not, are you concerned that you do not understand your player's business and are nervous about coaching your player?
- Do you feel like you have to impress your player with your knowledge or wit? Are you working at being clever and smart?
- Are you a seasoned, successful coach who can coach even with your eyes closed and one hand behind your back?
- Do you prefer doing the talking during a coaching session?
- Do you dread it when players talk about something extremely personal in their life, i.e., marriage, children, illness, death, fears, sex, religion, politics, etc.? Have you rehearsed in your mind a quick answer to move on to another subject?
- Are you so familiar with your players that you know what they're going to say before they say it?
- Do you have your agenda that you're determined to cover during the coaching session, regardless if it matches your player's agenda?
- Do you interrupt your player to tell a story that reminds you of this situation? Do you neglect to return to what the player was discussing?

- When your player is speaking, do you sometimes think, "Yada, yada, yada; yeah, yeah, yeah, enough already?"
- Do you have expectations of your client that you wouldn't dare to expect of yourself?
- Do you get bored with your player and mentally go out to lunch or doze off only to be awakened by your client asking a question that requires an intelligent response, such as "What do you think?"
- Are you threatened by the thought of players trusting you as a coach?
- Your player has done something that has upset you. Do you communicate your upset to the player or hold it in? Do you hold grudges against your player?

Look over your answers for a moment. Do you see traps where you are captured by something other than the player?

These points were designed to help you focus your attention. Interestingly enough, over the years we have discovered that, from time to time, even seasoned, successful coaches all fall into the trap of having their attention on themselves.

Whether you're just beginning your coaching career or have been around the block a few times, as we have, the key is to discover when you've checked out, or potential checking-out points, so you can get your attention back on the player.

> *Those who see the invisible do the impossible.*
> —quoted by Charlene Bernal, source unknown

Lend Me Your Ear— What Coaches Listen *For*

What do coaches listen for when their players are speaking? Coaches listen for the reasons, excuses, explanations, and stories as contrasted with dialogue that is headed toward actions which will produce intended outcomes. Wow, that's a mouthful. Let's take a closer look at what we just said.

Referring to the Go The Distance! coaching model in Chapter 2, we have discovered that what keeps players from reaching their goals (intended results) are all the reasons, excuses, explanations, and stories of why something cannot be done. Remember we said that people are mesmerized by activity? Staying busy and not going anyplace is an excuse.

People get too involved with the drama in life and are quick to say the reasons they can't do something. You've probably heard hundreds of the best.

Time is always wanting to me, and I cannot meet with a single day
when I am not hurried along, driven to my wit's-end by urgent work,
business to attend to, or some service to provide.
—George Sand, *Letters of George Sand*

Here's a beauty we recently heard:

"I couldn't get together with the other team members because of the renovation in the computer room and the racket. You just can't think with all those people coming and going; then if that weren't enough, I've had the air conditioning duct above me on full blast while the work's going on. Brrr. So I tried to keep busy going back and forth to the copy machine for each job rather than waiting until I have a number of things to photocopy. Then, of course, I just sneeze and sneeze; of course, that makes me have to go to the rest room for tissues. Of course, then I normally duck my head into the coffee room. What a mess. It takes a good two hours to clean it every day. You know, there's just not enough time in the day. I'm so busy. So you can understand why I wasn't able to attend the team meetings on a regular basis."

While you may not have come up against this type of player, they're out there and their excuses can be ingenious.

The excuses are the opposite of dialogue leading to actions that produce intended outcomes.

What would you do with our pal, "the sneezer?" In this scenario, a coach acknowledges the obstacles and works with the player to discover different ways or opportunities for the player to stay in action. In the case just mentioned, the coach may ask if it's possible to move from that location during construction, or call the facilities department to have the air conditioning vent changed. The solution may be as simple as asking that everyone in the office take turns being responsible for the coffee room.

As a coach, be mindful that it's your job to distinguish between the two dialogues in which the player is engaged. Is it a dialogue for activity or one for action? You can coach the player through the muck of activity into action.

The secret of joy in work is contained in one word—excellence.
To know how to do something well is to enjoy it.
—Pearl S. Buck, *The Joy of Children*

Will You Be Mine?
How to Engage the Player

In our years of coaching everyone from executives of Fortune 100 companies to teams to individuals to groups of volunteers to one-on-one sessions, along with our share of teenagers and children, we have collected methods to engage players.

These tools make it easier for players to listen to us. Remember that engage also means to fascinate, charm, captivate, engross, interest, absorb, allure, excite, enamor, enrapture, enthrall, enchant, mesmerize, delight, dazzle, occupy, involve, put into gear, clinch, connect, bind, and hook.

20 Ways to Engage Players

1. Have something the players want or need.
2. Introduce new concepts and ideas.
3. Challenge the player's thinking or beliefs.
4. Present facts.
5. Behave dramatically. Use props; dress in costume.
6. Tell one on yourself (even while it's happening). This takes away the notion that you have all the answers and do everything perfectly.
7. Use visual displays whenever the opportunity allows for it.
8. Use the name your player likes to be called.
9. Listen to your player and be interested.
10. Ask questions.
11. Keep a question open, like an inquiry.
12. Show that you know something about them/their business/their situation.
13. Direct your message to that which the player already has on his or her mind.
14. Be passionate about something.

15. Use examples from your life, don't be afraid this will diminish the player's respect for you.
16. Invite examples from the players' lives.
17. Use humor to make specific points; it's powerful.
18. Use games. Make a game out of accomplishing weekly results. Invite the players to take the significance and heaviness out and just go for it.
19. Demonstrate commitment to your player's well being.
20. Have fun!

I only wish I could find an institute that teaches people how to listen. After all, a good manager needs to listen at least as much as he needs to talk. Too many people fail to realize that real communication goes in both directions.
—Lee Iacocca

What's Your Mood?
Have You Ever Noticed That Your Moods Affect the Actions You Take and the Decisions you Make?

Keith Tang is a team leader for an aircraft company in Seattle. We began talking about moods and coaching during a break at a recent workshop. He said, "Boy, let me tell you about yesterday. I woke up and it was pouring. I grumbled, 'Another day of rain,' then had a cup of coffee and watched mystified as my tiny daughter belly-crawled across the carpet. I thought, 'Ah, the miracle of life.' Then my mood changed as I sat in gridlock on the way to work and again when I got to the office only to discover that my assistant had solved three problems before I even walked through the door. I had all these moods before eight a.m., and I didn't even think until right now that another swirled through as I looked in the rearview mirror to see my sparse hair getting sparser."

We all experience various moods throughout the day. There are probably things you can relate to in Keith's statement.

Have you caught yourself experiencing several moods while reading this book? One thing you can always count on is that at any moment there's a mood you're experiencing. Just as you experience a mood, so does your player.

Moods affect the way we listen to each other. If you're enthusiastic, you listen with ears of eagerness and your zest is reflected in your responses. It's the same way if you're bored, curious, distracted, or upset.

Have you ever come home from work after a monster day to find a surprise? Maybe it's a call on your answering machine from that person you've been hoping would call. Maybe it's your tax refund check. Maybe it's your loved ones giving you a hug. Your mood makes a difference in how you behave and especially how you listen.

Take a moment and look at the two models that follow. At first glance, they may look identical, but look closer. One is for the coach and the other for his or her player. The models represent the swirl of moods that occur within us. The moods rarely go on in sync; that is, your player may not feel reserved or curious when you are.

When you make the world tolerable for yourself, you make a world tolerable for others.
—Anais Nin

Be aware that your player is thinking and feeling a myriad of emotions when you're talking and coaching. To think otherwise is foolhardy.

Joy Jones, a planner for an E-commerce accounting company in the Rockies, had a Thunderbolt! when we shared these models. She said, "This swirl of moods is like the summer weather in Colorado. It's ever changing." That's a perfect analogy.

Don't be afraid to give up the good to go for the great.
—Kenny Rogers, singer

Are you aware that if you suspect a player's mood that is not forwarding the action, you can cause a change in mood by asking appropriate questions?

If you find yourself in a mood that isn't sufficient for the task at hand in coaching (say you're distracted because your car made weird sounds as you drove in), use the model to help generate a mood to forward your commitment. These models are designed to heighten your listening skills further.

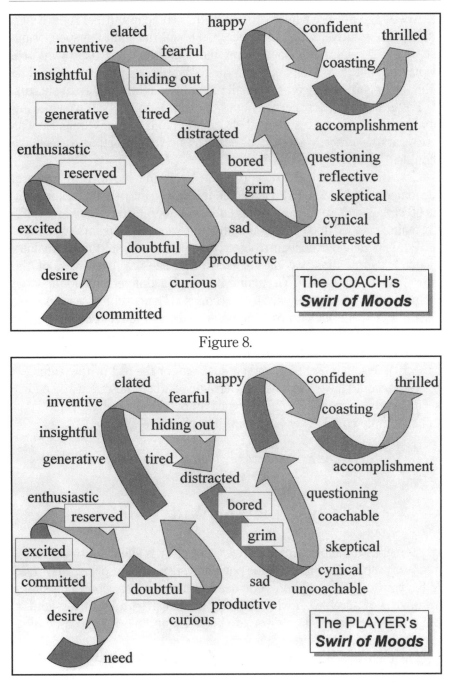

Figure 8.

Figure 9.

About a year ago, while working with a company in Tel Aviv, Kevin Miller, an executive, said, "I'm concerned about the team I'm sponsoring. The team is adamant about doing the redesign work their way." He explained that they were not using the tools we trained them to use. The other eight corporate teams were all using these tools with great success.

Kevin was justly concerned about the team's progress. It was moving at a snail's pace. The team members couldn't agree on anything. He was told that the process seemed useless. Days were starting to feel like months.

Germaine was asked to un-stick the team and move them forward. Germaine says, "It was odd. The moment I walked into a team meeting, my mood changed. It went from being enthusiastic to being heavy and dull." Germaine stopped, took a deep breath and reviewed the team's objectives.

While reviewing the team's objectives, there was a shift in Germaine's mood. "The attention was off the coach and back to the success of the effort." What happened? Germaine invented a different mood, and the intentional mood change only took seconds. "The coaching session went great. I got them back on track, empowered them to choose and use the tools we trained them to use. They were the first team to present their findings to the executives. Not only that, they set a standard of professionalism, crispness in presenting, and enthusiasm for the rest of the teams."

What would have happened if Germaine hadn't interceded and hadn't seen that the mood of the team needed an overhaul? As Kevin said later, "They simply could never have met their objectives."

> *The quieter you become, the more you can hear.*
> —Baba Ram Dass

Just Listen, Will You?

Sometimes the best gift you give to a player is silence.

As you coach, learn to use the power of silence. All a player may need is for you to listen and nod your head, indicating that you understand. You may not agree with what is being said or even fully understand it, but a nod lets players know you are listening and receiving communication. This can be very freeing for the player.

There have been many times when we just listened. We nodded our heads. We maintained eye contact. We were there and receptive to communication.

> *It takes two to speak the truth—one to speak, and another to hear.*
> —Henry David Thoreau

Are you unsure when silence is your best tool to use? It has a lot of uses, yet from our experience, it's usually when a player is frustrated.

To be sure, you might just want to ask your player, "Do you want me to just listen to what you have to say or do you want my input?" In fact, we advocate training your players to let you know when they want you to just listen to them. We have clients call us and say, "I'm having a bad day. Will you just listen?" Most times, these phone calls will last three to five minutes. As coaches, we're listening to free up the players.

Larry Lamb, a national accounts sales manager for McCormick and Company, was in one of our CoachLabs. "I find what helps me to listen better when talking to one of my brokers is to count to four before responding. That way, if there's anything else they'd like to say, I give them that opportunity."

> *I listen and give input only if somebody asks.*
> —Barbara Bush, former First Lady
> of the United States and humanitarian

Summary

Listening is an essential tool for your coaching toolkit. It's a skill you can learn. With listening, the focus of a coaching session is on the player and not the coach.

Players and coaches each experience a plethora of possible moods. The key is to know that the swirl of moods is like the weather, ever-changing. It can and does affect the way we listen.

In the next chapter, we'll focus on you and building your confidence. It's time to have you consider your coaching philosophy. It's easy. It's fun. And you'll find it helpful as you wear the hat of a coach.

CHAPTER 8

*There's an element of truth in every idea that lasts long
enough to be called corny.*
—Irving Berlin

YOUR COACHING PHILOSOPHY

Outcomes of this chapter:
- Use a coaching philosophy to focus your work.
- Build your self-esteem.
- Write your Coaching Biography.

In this chapter, you'll have a chance to contemplate and consider. Sound like odd tools for your coaching toolkit? They could be the best ones of the bunch because when you finish reading this chapter and doing the exercises, you should feel grounded in your coaching philosophy. If you're not quite there, you'll know what needs work in order to achieve your objective: to be an effective coach.

If you flip to Webster's Dictionary to discover the meaning of philosophy, you'll find a range of definitions. For our purposes, we are using the term philosophy to mean a particular system of principles for the conduct of life.

Now, in that definition, just swap life with coaching. In coaching, what are the principles or beliefs you have and use? Perhaps, like many coaches, and especially those who are in the early stages, you have yet to form a philosophy. We applaud you because you're going to start with a strong foundation of beliefs and have the opportunity to develop more. Here's our coaching philosophy. We hope it helps to open your pathway.

Our Philosophy

1. Effective coaches are made, not born. Effective coaching can be learned.
2. Players are, from the beginning, capable and able. They may not know it yet.
3. Coaching is crucial to performance excellence.
4. Anyone who wants to be an effective coach can be. It isn't hard or difficult.
5. Coaches learn from and with their players. The coaching relationship is a learn/learn situation.
6. It is a privilege to be someone's coach.
7. The coaching relationship is a sacred and confidential one.
8. Players provide the primary commitment and enthusiasm to achieve their objectives. Coaches facilitate and augment those necessary components.

We hope that sharing our philosophy with you will begin to jog your mind in articulating what your philosophy is.

It is a common experience that a problem difficult at night is resolved in the morning after the committee of sleep has worked on it.
—John Steinbeck

Philosophy? Why Have One?

Whether you're coaching the Seattle Seahawks or the Mayberry Maybugs, you have a coaching philosophy. For those who are about to coach a team, a client, or the kids, the philosophy may be fuzzy.

Your philosophy is the basis from which you work, from which all your ideas and motivations arise. It's why you do and say the things that you do. It's the result of experience and wisdom. It is a way of being. Your coaching philosophy will impact that area. It shapes your thoughts and actions.

Remember to put your oxygen mask on first before helping other passengers.
—Continental Airlines Flight Attendant

Don't take our word for it. Write out your coaching philosophy, and notice what happens in the days that follow. Articulating and bringing clarity to what your coaching philosophy is will validate your past actions or produce new actions and a new way of thinking. Just try it.

Philosophical statements need not be lengthy to be inspirational and powerful, or even exciting. Here are two short quotes that are examples of philosophy, albeit not directly related to coaching, that we find uplifting.

"My mother once told me I could either be smart or pleasant. I tried smart for a number of years. I recommend pleasant." (Elwood P. Dowd, played by James Stewart in the play and the movie, *Harvey* by Mary Beth Chase).

"May I always be the kind of person my dog thinks I am." *(The Pickwick Papers Company)*

Now it's your turn. Take a sheet of paper and try this exercise.

EXERCISE:

1. List at least two people who coached, advised, or mentored you and made a positive difference in your results. You needn't have liked them, but reflect about what you admired or respected in these people.
2. Write down their attributes or characteristics and actions that made them effective in this role.
3. From this, write your own coaching philosophy and style. It is important that you write it out. You'll want to study *it*, revise *it*, and polish *it* until *it* says exactly who you are as a coach.

I Was Born... Your Coaching Biography

If you're serious about helping others to succeed at anything, to share your coaching skills, read this section carefully. All of the components of the coaching biography, or this tool, may not fit your specific application; however, we urge you to write out your biography. Doing so will help clarify your coaching ideas and abilities for yourself. This is a powerful tool.

We've trained thousands of people in the skills of writing their coaching biography. For those men and women who are in the arena of professional business coaching, the application is immediately visible. Sometimes, however, for those who don't want to be professional coaches, the idea seems too vague. Please don't fall for that myth. This is an invaluable exercise for you and a powerful tool to use.

The biography tells others who you are, where you've been, and the types of results that you've produced. The biography (bio for short) is unlike a resume in that a bio is structured and written in a broader context than a resume. The names of clients are kept confidential, but the bio boasts their accomplishments as a reflection of the coach.

Review the following examples before you begin writing your own. Let's review each section of the biography as you also glance at the samples that follow.

Name, address and phone number: As you can see, we recommend centering this across the top of the page. Include your e-mail address and website, if you have them. This information should be your most recent "reach numbers" for people to contact you.

Specialization: This section is a summary of your skills, experience, and talent. This is an area where you can say what you like to do, what you're good at doing, where you've been, etc.

Experience: This is the section where you write specifics about projects on which you've worked or jobs you've had. List your accomplishments and clients' accomplishments here. What were they? If you've had jobs that shed light on your expertise, include them in this section. The main thrust here is to list your accomplishments that have, because of your participation as a coach, enabled certain achievements to come about. (Look at the examples.)

Education/Background: List your education, degrees and awards earned, any certifications, special training, etc. We recommend giving some background about yourself, i.e., hobbies, volunteer work, interests, family, etc. This makes you a real person, not just a list upon a sheet of paper.

Strive to keep your biography to one page. If you must exceed that, make it no longer than a page and a half.

At one page, the bio is more inviting to read and takes seconds for a quick glance. A one-page bio isn't an arduous document that one must sit down, concentrate on, and possibly muddle through with lists and topics. People are busy. We like things in a nutshell or news bite.

A few of our clients/coaches have their bio on one side of the sheet and a list of services on the other. It looks good and works great as a handout. Further, consider having your photo printed on the bio.

Sort out what best represents you and the message you want left with those you meet. Then write your bio.

Exhibit F

John R. Tough
2314 Peach Boulevard
New Orleans , LA 23457
(504) 555-9876   FAX (504) 555-9877
jrtough@eaglesview.com

SPECIALIZATION-

John's distinguished record of national and international business achievement provides him with the experience and understanding to coach executives, managers, and entrepreneurs in producing extraordinary results. He also leads workshops in leadership and performance. John demonstrates a remarkable commitment to his clients' growth and outstanding results.

EXPERIENCE-

John's clients have produced some impressive business results including one Fortune 500 business unit's ROCE improving from a -1% to +19% in two years; and a small, eight-year-old engineering firm doubling their revenues in one year.

John's business career spans thirty years. He has served as President of the International Group for Acme & Western Industries. John expanded A&WI's market share 347% in seven years. He also served as Group Vice President and General Manager for Federal-Morales Corporation and Manager of Latin American operations for American Lumber Corporation, tripling their gross revenues in four years.

John has lived and worked in Europe and Latin America, speaks fluent Spanish, and has traveled extensively in the Pacific and Far East.

EDUCATION / BACKGROUND-

John holds an M.B.A. from Stanford University's Graduate School of Business and an A.B. in Economics-Accountancy, also from Stanford. He was All University Boxing Champion at Stanford, winning the Gene Tunney Golden Glove.

John, a certified enterprise coach, received his formal organizational coaching training from Eagle's View Systems in Kingwood, Texas.

A US Marine Corps veteran, John was a helicopter pilot serving in Vietnam. He and his wife, Mary, enjoy tennis, bicycling, and golf. Their three children, Jane, Dick and Harry, all practice medicine.

Exhibit G

Mary S. Bright
7 Ashwood Court
Carmel, CA 95876
(408) 555- 5764   FAX (408) 555-5765
msbright@eaglesview.net

SPECIALIZATION-

Mary is a professional business coach for small business owners and managers, helping them grow and develop their enterprises. She coaches in a wide variety of industries, including real estate, building and contracting, healthcare, retail sales, and the arts. Mary has practiced in functional areas such as sales, marketing, and operations. Her focus with business owners has been to facilitate creating their business vision and the development of strategies to fulfill that vision.

EXPERIENCE-

Mary has successfully owned and operated her own small business for 12 years. She measures her success by her clients' results, which include:

• Retail/wholesale furniture store increased sales in one year to their highest level in nine years while improving the bottom line 50%.

• Real estate sales client improved productivity 257% in one year.

• Art gallery client expanded their showroom and improved revenue 76% in six months.

EDUCATION / BACKGROUND-

Mary has been formally educated in coaching from several institutions, including the Coaches Training Institute, San Rafael, California and the Center for Professional Development , Scottsdale, Arizona, studying management, team building, and marketing. She is a certified coach for the time transformation course, Eagle's View: TAKING OFF!

Mary is a registered Dental Hygenist, holding an A.S. degree in Dental Hygiene from Lane College, Eugene, Oregon. She is also certified in massage through the Twin Lakes College of the Healing Arts, Los Angeles, California.

Mary enjoys dance, photography, and health and fitness activities.

More Helpful Hints

Look over the following words as you write your biography. A Yale University study found the following are the ten most persuasive words in the English language.

We recommend that you use them as much as possible.

The Ten Most Persuasive Words:

YOU
DISCOVER
NEW
PROVEN
EASY
RESULTS
SAVE
LOVE
GUARANTEE
MONEY

Okay. You caught us. Yes, we used these words whenever we could throughout the book. We also suggest using strong verbs. Scan the list that follows, and mark the words that you may want to use in writing your coaching biography or the other materials that you generate as part of your coaching experience and work.

Exhibit H

Use **STRONG VERBS**

Scan the list below and mark the words that strike you as words you may want to use in writing your Coaching Biography. This is only a partial list. Refer to a Dictionary and Thesaurus as well.

Advised	Eliminated	Operated	Revised
Advocated	Enabled	Orchestrated	Scheduled
Analyzed	Established	Ordered	Scored
Architected	Evaluated	Organized	Selected
Assembled	Expanded	Persuaded	Served
Audited	Extracted	Piloted	Set up
Built	Forced	Planned	Sold
Budgeted	Formulated	Practiced	Solidified
Calculated	Founded	Predicted	Solved
Captured	Generated	Prepared	Sorted
Classified	Guided	Presented	Spoke
Coached	Handled	Processed	Started
Communicated	Hired	Produced	Streamlined
Compiled	Identified	Programmed	Studied
Conducted	Illustrated	Projected	Summarized
Configured	Implemented	Proposed	Supervised
Constructed	Improved	Proved	Supplied
Consulted	Increased	Provided	Surveyed
Converted	Inspected	Purchased	Taught
Coordinated	Installed	Recommended	Traced
Created	Instructed	Reconciled	Tracked
Defined	Interviewed	Recruited	Trained
Delivered	Invented	Redesigned	Translated
Demonstrated	Investigated	Reduced	Trimmed
Designed	Lectured	Referred	Tripled
Detected	Led	Reorganized	Unified
Developed	Maintained	Reported	Upgraded
Diagnosed	Managed	Represented	Verified
Directed	Mediated	Researched	Won
Discovered	Monitored	Resolved	Worked
Distributed	Negotiated	Reviewed	Wrote

This is only a partial list. Refer to a dictionary and thesaurus as well.

One of our clients, Peggy Richards, felt like she didn't have the right qualifications to call herself a coach. The first assignment Germaine gave her was to write a biography.

After much deliberation and the completion of her homework, she met with Germaine. Before their meeting, Peggy had several people read what she had written and got some powerful feedforward.

When Germaine and Peggy completed reviewing the bio, Peggy felt renewed and empowered. She said, "To tell you the truth, Germaine, I thought the idea was rather convoluted. Actually, I wondered if it was some type of coaching psycho-babble. But now, I get it. I can see, here in black and white, my accomplishments. I feel proud because I realized all the experience and training I have will make a difference in coaching people."

To top that, her biography helped grow her business. Potential clients were impressed with what they read and wanted her to coach them! We shouted, "Way to go, Peggy!"

We have discovered that when you write your own bio, it has the effect of enlivening you and building your self-esteem and confidence.

Summary

Our hope is that, as you finish this chapter, you've gained more clarity regarding your coaching philosophy. We like to say that a coaching philosophy is the context from whence coaching originates.

Writing your coaching biography increases your self-esteem. It is a tool to use for prospecting. It serves as a reminder to your clients of who you are. Additionally, your biography is something they can share with their friends about their coach.

In our next chapter, we offer ways to understand the coaching "value drift," along with methods to measure your coaching effectiveness. We show how to invent meaningful coaching performance indicators and how to utilize a Coaching Call Plan Checklist to ensure Thunderbolt! coaching and continuity.

Chapter 9

Keep in mind that the true meaning of an individual is how he treats a person who can do him absolutely no good.
—Ann Landers

THE COACH'S VALUE

Outcomes of this chapter:
- Encounter a model disclosing how players assess your value.
- Uncover the phenomenon of the "value drift," and learn how to manage it successfully.
- Discover new ways to measure your coaching effectiveness, and expand your coaching ability.
- Learn how to invent meaningful coaching performance indicators for yourself that improve your coaching.
- Acquire/invent a Coaching Call Plan Checklist to ensure quality coaching and continuity.

Let's say you are a coach with a number of players you are actively coaching. Let's say, once again, you ask your players how valuable your coaching is. What do you suppose each would say?

Predictably, each player's answer would be somewhat different. TJ may rate your value as quite high. Drake might rate you "mediocre, but with potential." Bette might report that you're the best thing since sliced bread. Doreen may not want to answer at all.

How would you assess your coach's value? Where would you find the answers?

In not making the decision, you've made one.
Not doing something is the same as doing it.
—Ivan Bloch

Rating Your Value

We believe that while each player may give you a different score, the method of scoring or rating is fundamentally the same. Players want results. They don't want a new best friend or someone who merely cheers from the sidelines. They want help, and they want it fast and easy, too. When asked, they consciously or unconsciously look at the desired outcomes produced in relation to your coaching.

The highest form of "in relation to your coaching" is to have a player attribute extraordinary results to you, the coach. Study the Coach's Value model in Figure 10 for a moment, and let's look at the meanings of the words used to score the coach.

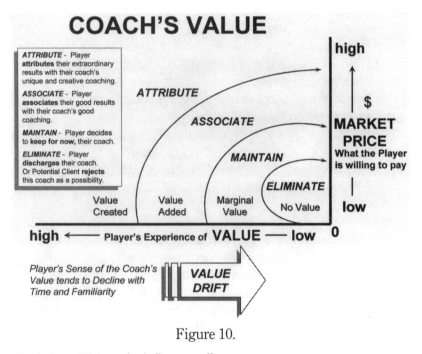

Figure 10.

Here's how Webster's defines attribute:

at-trib-ute ñ verb. 1. Produced by, resulting from, arising from or originating in; to credit. 2. To assign or ascribe cause. 3. To think of as the source of. 4. To consider or indicate as a creator of. 5. Accredit.

When a player attributes results to the coach, it is a strong endorsement. This is the player who might say, "I couldn't have done it without my coach!" The player considers his or her coach to be a "value creator," someone who supplied the ability to invent things that generate value (thus, it's value-created). This coach is regarded as unique and brilliantly resourceful. This player would definitely give the coach referrals. The player would undoubtedly consider the investment of time and money well spent.

The next level down from attribute is to associate.

as-so-ci-ate ñ verb. 1. To connect or bring together in the mind or imagination. 2. To link or relate; correlate. 3. Following or accompanying. - noun. Ally, cohort, partner, colleague.

While not as profound a relationship to your coaching as attribute, associate is quite strong and far stronger than maintain. As coaches, our value to our clients is in their minds and imaginations. It is a matter of experience, perception, and interpretation. For us to be successful in the long-term, our players must link or relate their favorable results to our coaching efforts. Coaches are regarded as an ally and partner when the players associate good results with us. We are considered to be value added. That is to say, our work with them is perceived as adding value in the service of helping them to achieve their objectives.

Let's see what we mean by the level of maintain.

main-tain ñ verb. 1. To continue or carry on. 2. Keep up; preserve; sustain.

In the area designated maintain, the player is not yet pleased with the results linked to our coaching. The player perceives marginal or little value from the coaching experience at this time. It may be that the player sees no correlation between their positive results and the coaching that has occurred.

We assert that it is the coach's responsibility to point out, if necessary, the linkages or connections between the player's accomplishments and the coaching. As you remember from the beginning of the book, humans are not particularly coachable in the first place. One of our human blind spots is giving others credit for their successes. Sometimes we have to help them a little.

Okay, we're not fired yet. Our player is willing to wait and see. But for how long? How long is she or he willing to pay the price without some pleasing outcomes or payback in relation to our coaching? How long will our player be willing to maintain us as coach? How long will the player tolerate a lack of positive results before their perception of us slides to eliminate?

> **e-lim-i-nate** ñ verb. 1. To get rid of; remove. 2. To leave out or omit from consideration; reject. 3. Eradicate, liquidate, purge, discharge. 4. Do away with; put to an end.

Here, the player is sufficiently displeased with the results in relation to our coaching to dismiss the coaching services. Eliminate in our model also includes prospects or potential clients as well as existing players.

Truth Is Stranger than Fiction— Know the Truth About Coaching

As a coach, it's time you knew the truth: When the coach's rates or fees are quite low, the coach's possible value may be perceived as low. The coach may wonder why he or she is not being hired and may say something like, "I don't understand it; my fees are lower than anyone else's out there and in some cases, one-third of what some coaches are charging. Yet, these people are getting all the business and I am struggling. What am I doing wrong?"

Perhaps it is only a matter of perception on the part of the prospective players. Perceived low value is associated with low fees. It is actually possible to generate higher perceived value merely by increasing your fees.

Once, Germaine was meeting with Phil Barron, one of her players, at his client's headquarters in Tulsa, Oklahoma. One of Phil's direct reports, Anita, was in the meeting with them, and she said, "Phil, I'd like to hire Doug Doe to coach me in this project."

Phil was surprised but didn't miss a beat. "Okay. But I am not clear here. Why don't you have Germaine coach you?"

She replied, "Because Mr. Doe charges a lot less than Germaine does. No offense, Germaine."

"None taken," Germaine replied.

Phil hesitated a moment, and Germaine remembers him pursing his lips before he said, "Anita, consider the possibility that one hour with Germaine is worth more than a whole day with Doug Doe, and that explains the difference in their fees."

Jed reports, "It's happened so often, I know it's true. The more my clients pay, the better they listen and the greater their results."

As the coach's fees rise toward the high range, the coach's player market will shift. The coach's market may expand, contract, or even disappear when fees are raised.

For example, when Jed managed his life insurance agency, he developed a reputation in the Seattle area as being one of the best recruiters around and tops in new agent retention.

One day Jed's friend, John, said, "You're so darn good at this recruiting/retention game, you ought to put on a seminar. You could teach other general agents and managers how to do what you do. I'd pay to learn how to do what you do, and I'm certain everybody else in town would too."

So, Jed and his colleague, Bill, designed a two-day workshop and began inviting agency managers and supervisors to attend.

One of the first people Jed called was his friend, John, who had suggested the workshop. John said, "It sounds great, and I'd love to come— but not for $150."

"Well, you know, John, since it was your idea..."

John interrupted, "I'll come for $500."

"Excuse me?"

"I said I would come for $500 not $150. For $150 it can't be worth my time. But for $500, I know *there* has got to be value *there*!" John said.

Naturally, it was too late to increase the price for the people who had already signed up. But it wasn't too late to tell them that the next time they had the seminar, it would be priced at $500. Jed recalls the response to that comment. People said, "Five-hundred dollars! Man, you must be really giving people the goods in that seminar!"

The Value Drift

We've observed that the player's sense of the coach's value naturally declines over time. We call this perceptual decline the "value drift." There

As the coach/player relationship becomes more comfortable, the player stops distinguishing the coaching value that is present. After a time, the coaching can become almost transparent or taken for granted. The presence disappears into the background. The familiarity of it literally makes it harder to distinguish.

Here's an analogy of the value drift. We're sure you have one of your own.

Jed says, "When I was eight, my family and I moved from Los Angeles to Longview, Washington. As we drove near the outskirts of the town, I got a whiff of a pulp mill for the first time. I didn't like it at all; and if you've ever had that experience, you can understand. That's one strong smell. So, from the backseat of the family station wagon, I shared my thoughts with my family as only an eight-year old can, comparing it to everything from dirty socks to the fumes in the kitchen when Mom cooked broccoli. Mom and my sister, Carolyn, made a fuss, too. Yet the strangest thing happened. After only about 30 minutes, the offensive odor disappeared for everyone. I remember Mom asking, 'What happened to the awful odor, Ed? Where did it go?' and my father replied, 'Smell? What smell?'"

Familiarity contributes to the decline of the player's perception of the coach's value. The coach's value becomes transparent.

> *The important thing is to learn a lesson every time you lose.*
> —John McEnroe

As the player becomes more effective, confidence increases. The player becomes more willing to trust his or her own abilities. This desirable self-confidence can also contribute to the decline of the player's attributing or associating the favorable results associated with coaching.

It may happen that the player's confidence grows into over-confidence, which could be considered as arrogance. An arrogant player considers that he or she has created the results and no longer needs the coach. It's presumed that the coach is all used up. The player thinks that no new insights or new openings for action are possible from the coach/player relationship.

None of the above is meant to suggest or imply that the player cannot wake up and appreciate the coach's value. The player can at any instant become aware for any variety of reasons. But time and familiarity are silent, powerful, yet gentle currents flowing in the opposite direction. The natural drift is for the player to cease distinguishing the coach's value. It is a natural drift even to the point that the player may suspect the coach is "just happy to go along for the ride."

Now that you're aware of this natural value drift, you can anticipate it and not feel shocked when it comes. The value drift is just part of the human condition. Be on the lookout for it so you can deal with it effectively. Great coaches embrace it as part of their profession. As Kelsey Lauren, a coach we met from Philadelphia, said, "It's just an occupational hazard to be managed."

Your #1 priority is to have your player win. It remains important that players could be losing a lot when they no longer recognize the coach's value. If this happens, the player may stop using the coach effectively, and that can hurt the player's results markedly.

The road to failure is often decorated by the flowers of past achievements.
—Socrates

Of course, "winning" for your player might mean that you'll be out of a job, too. If you're effective, the player will no longer need you. In fact, that might be every great coach's dream!

In business, as in life, we all need a purpose beyond ourselves
to feel useful, worthwhile and good about ourselves.
—Charles Handy, *The Age of Unreason*

Your Happy Ending—
Working Yourself Out of a Job

Be aware that players may become coach-dependent. Coaching should always be developmental. The bottom line is that our mission is to work our way out of a job. We tell our players that right up front, whether they are individuals or teams.

Recently, our client, Ralph Hedges, asked us to "shadow" an internal consultant whom we had trained to lead one of our programs. There was some concern that Jackie might not be as effective as we would be, and it was important to have the best in this case. The training and coaching program would be conducted with six teams of people from one of Ralph's company's newest foreign acquisitions.

This would be the first real exposure that the acquired employees would have of their new owners. Ralph and the other executives thought it was imperative to make a good first impression with this training. We were asked to co-lead with Jackie during the second and third training sessions. They were confident Jackie could handle the first session with adequate support from two of their vice presidents and general managers. However, they were worried about the second and third sessions. Those sessions might be another story.

A few days later, after Jackie had led the first session, we received a call from our client, Ralph. "Remember the work in Germany that we wanted you to do with Jackie? Well, the good news is, you have done such an outstanding job of training and coaching Jackie that we won't need you anymore; and the bad news is, you just lost some billing. Sorry, Jed and Germaine."

In fact, we were delighted. Mission accomplished. We had worked our way out of a job.

Taking Good Care— How to Manage the Value Drift

Here are some tips on managing the value drift:

1. Count on it happening. It is a question of when, not if, your player's appreciation of your value will slip. By the way, there is no such drift in a positive direction. A good metaphor here is the law of atrophy: Everything is headed in the direction of falling apart. Watch for the value drift. Stay alert.
2. Be authentically committed to your player's success. If you can't be, you'll both fail.
3. Have integrity. Tell the truth. Don't expect to be told the truth. Do what you say you will do by when you say you will do it.
4. Tell your players about the value drift, and tell them that it's natural. They need to know it's not a problem for you.
5. Ask your players to help manage the value drift. Have them be responsible for building a case for your value as coach. Have them see that it is to their benefit to do so.

6. Make it a practice to acknowledge every positive result that your player produces.
7. At every coaching session have your players tell you what's working in the accomplishment of their objectives as well as what isn't working. This provides an opening for them to mention your coaching. It is much more effective than fishing for compliments. If you find your player fishing for compliments, reread number 6.
8. Pay attention to your player's learning style. Make sure your player gets what is needed the way the player learns best.
9. Study the tools of coaching and continue to practice your skills. Learn as much as you can, even if you currently believe you know all the tricks of the trade. Take our word for it, there are new tools available every day. Why? You'll be rejuvenated by your study and find yourself feeling fresh in your coaching sessions. Your players will be hard put to accuse you of ever being stale.
10. Be creative! Be willing to take risks with your coaching. Don't be afraid to try new, outrageous methods and techniques. Don't be brainless or foolhardy either.

The Coach's Value Model can help you determine your near-term approach or strategy with your player.

Ethics is about what is right, not who is right.
—quoted by Eva Shaw, Ph.D., *author, source unknown*

What's the Number, Please?
Measuring the Coach's Effectiveness

Most coaches will tell you that they measure their own success by the success of their players. It is the ultimate objective for coaches to have their players win.

Is that the only measure of a coach's effectiveness? Isn't it a little late at the end of the game to see if you were on the right track? Wouldn't you rather have some tools available along the way to tell you if you're on or off course? Would it be helpful to have techniques to see if you're effective or need to make some changes?

Let's think about the key performance indicators for coaches. What are they? We've asked this question to hundreds of trainers and coaches.

Here is a sampling of the responses:

Performance Indicators for Measuring Coaches:

1. Players are positively challenged by the coach.
2. Players keep their agreements with the coach.
3. Players do what they say they will do when they say they'll do it.
4. Players apply what they learn from coaching sessions.
5. Players are observably "in action" regarding their commitments and objectives.
6. Players leave coaching sessions inspired and enthusiastic.
7. The players inspire the coach.
8. Others comment about the positive results that the players produce.
9. Players give the coach referrals.
10. Players give the coach unsolicited thanks, or other demonstrations of appreciation.
11. The coach learns from the players.
12. The players are winning. They are accomplishing their milestones and objectives.
13. What you see happening with players is consistent with your Coaching Philosophy.
14. The coach is thinking from the future, out ahead of the players.

Excellence is the result of caring more than others think is wise, risking more than others think is safe, dreaming bigger than others think is practical and promising more than others think is possible.
—quoted by Chris Bernal, *management consultant, source unknown*

How to Invent Performance Indicators

You will also find this discussion useful in assisting your players in designing their objectives.

Here are ways in which you can consider performance:

- New Explicit Circumstances
- Distinctive Reactions
- Particular Consequences
- Specific Measurable Results
- Recurring Desirable Events
- Quantifiable Outcomes
- Descriptive Behaviors
- Definite Effects
- Special Achievements
- Prescribed Changes in Environment

Now, the first thing to know about inventing indicators, sometimes called measures or metrics, is that it is perfectly legitimate to do so. That is to say, you are perfectly welcome to make them up.

The ones that we are already familiar with, the measures that the world goes by, were all invented, too. Consider performance indicators or measures such as profit and loss, kilometers, miles, pounds, and ounces. All made up!

Long ago in a kingdom far, far away, an enterprising prince wondered how far the castle was from the forest. "It's over there," as a measurement just didn't work for him anymore.

The princess, always a step ahead of the prince, suggested, "Let's pace it off and then we'll know the distance."

The prince wasn't sure about this and examined his shoes before replying. "Look here. Your feet are smaller than mine. Everyone's pace will be different."

The princess, typically solution-oriented said, "We need a standard pace, a measurement, since not everyone's stride is the same."

So, they got the king to walk around the castle and determined his stride was "so long." We'll call this stride a 'yard' and declare it the official measure in the realm!" said the princess. Then the prince interrupted, "Hey, I have a Thunderbolt! While the king's outside, let's measure his foot..."

We've had fun making up this story, but the bottom line is that all measurements are invented. It is perfectly legitimate for you to invent them as well.

Your indicators can have the power to change the face of things, the power to change the game, whether the game is business or an athletic contest.

For instance, the 3-point shot in basketball was invented to make the game more interesting and increase attendance for the National Basketball Association in the United States. It did just that. It is possible that you could invent indicators that would make you more powerful as a coach.

Remember, all indicators measure something and are always quantifiable. These are examples of forms of quantification:

- number
- more of / less of
- percent or fraction
- ratio, proportion or balance
- happened / didn't happen
- time
- money
- existing / absent

As you can see, there are many forms of quantification. These examples may be a useful reference to help you invent your own Coaching Performance Indicators.

In any kind of measurement, numbers by themselves don't tell you anything. The story is told when the numbers are used in comparison. If Zelda, your player, reports that last week she produced 27, it doesn't tell you anything. But if Zelda says, "I produced 27 and my target was 25," a goal has been exceeded.

It is critical to create background or history with the indicators you're using. For instance, if your player, Milton, tells you he produced 36 against a target of 31, and no one in the office has hit 36 for two years, that tells you that 36 is even more significant than you might have thought. Well done, Milton!

An excellent place to look to help you invent Coaching Performance Indicators may be your coaching philosophy. Take time to consider the indicators used by your favorite coaches, mentors, and teachers. What characteristics and attributes did they possess that you admired? What things did they do that contributed to you and your team's success? Perhaps you can turn some of those things into indicators yourself.

EXERCISE:

Write down at least three ways that you would measure yourself as a coach. Feel free to consult the sample indicator lists, your coaching philosophy, or your list of attributes that your favorite coaches exemplified.

My Coaching Measures:

1. _____
2. _____
3. _____
4. _____
5. _____
6. _____

Notes: _____

Here's the Plan, Stan—
The Coaching Call Plan Checklist

We use the Coaching Call Plan Checklist before, during, and after each coaching session. We have it printed on cards that we carry with us. The checklist helps us to plan our coaching session before, and keeps us on track during, the time we invest with our player. The checklist is a good tool when used to plan coaching improvements.

As part of our Coaching Call Plan Checklist, we have included a section at the end, number 7, for the coach to measure his or her effectiveness during the coaching session. You may want to create your own checklist after you have adopted and/or invented the indicators you decide to use to measure your coaching effectiveness.

Exhibit I

Coaching Call Plan Checklist

1. Call objectives
2. Points to cover
3. (Check in) Openings
4. Promised results from last call status
5. Good questions to ask
6. Notes/Promises from this call
7. Call Effectiveness Checklist
   - Enthusiasm.
   - Inspiration. Openings for Action.
   - Ask more of the players than they would ordinarily ask of themselves.
   - Ask questions vs. tell or advise.
   - Thunderbolts!, Insights.
   - Other Effectiveness Indicators:

   _____

   _____

   _____

As you can see, there is a write-in section. This is for indicators we may want to use just for that session, new ones we've learned about, or those we've recently invented.

Those blanks make us aware that we should constantly be looking for new ways of measuring ourselves as coaches and helping our players.

> *If there is a better way to do it, find it.*
> —Thomas A. Edison

With a coach's magnifying glass in our hands, let's take a closer look at the Coaching Call Plan Checklist.

1. Call objectives

Determine your objectives for each coaching session or call. What are the outcomes that you want to have as a result of this dialogue with your player? For example, your objective might be to review your player's plans for the coming week or to help him or her solve a particular problem they've told you about. Whatever your objectives, write them out to make sure you are clear about them before your session. This helps to ensure that your coaching session will be effective.

2. Points to cover

In addition to your objectives for the call, organize other items you'll want to cover. This might include information you promised to get for a player/client or facts you must get from the player. An example here may be to confirm the date for a future event or give your player a phone number for a possible referral to his or her business.

3. Openings (check in)

Plan your opening dialogue with your players. Ordinarily, we like to check in with our player first. That is, we want to get into communication with our player through whatever is foremost on his or her mind at the moment. Of course, we have our agenda, and we'll get to it. First, we must encourage the player to listen. Remember, the coaching session may not be all that's going on in the player's brain. You can accomplish this by asking how the day has been or asking, "What's happening?" You may know the player's been on holiday, so you could start with, "How was your vacation?"

4. Promised results from last call status

Ask what was accomplished and what didn't get done with regard to the player's objectives since your last coaching conversation. Follow-up is a great service to your player; a lack of it communicates that promises aren't important.

5. Good questions to ask

This should be determined or guided by your objectives for the session.

6. Notes/Promises from this call

Most of what you'll want to record from your session will be the promises your player makes to you and any requests made of you. We have discovered over the years that little else is worth recording.

7. Call Effectiveness Checklist

As we mentioned earlier in this chapter, at the end of every coaching session, we stop, reflect, and rate our effectiveness as coaches. This checklist contains the things that we want to keep in mind that are important to effective coaching dialogue:

a. Enthusiasm — A certain amount of player enthusiasm always contributes to players achieving their objectives. A lack of player enthusiasm can be an important communication tool, too. It signals our next coaching move or suggests that we take time to reshape our coaching strategy. We also want to measure our own level of enthusiasm. If we find ourselves without sufficient enthusiasm about the player or his or her projects, we'd better generate it or get coaching ourselves to analyze the source of it being missing.

b. Inspiration. Openings for Action — Here, look to be inspired by your player. Sometimes we need to be inspiring for our player. At this checkpoint, note whether your player inspired you or if you provided inspiration when it was missing. When we do this reflection, we consider if our dialogue co-generated new possible actions for the player to take toward achieving objectives. If it did, we're doing our job.

c. Challenge — Ask more of the players than they would ordinarily ask of themselves.

The first step to having what you really want is the removal of everything in your environment that represents mediocrity, removing those things that are limiting. One way is to surround yourself with people who ask more of you than you do.
—Stewart Emery

And...

The most effective coaches we've known frequently ask more of their players than the players would ask of themselves.

As coaches, we may not want to do this on every coaching occasion, but we can be open to this possibility by confronting it on our checklist each time we coach.

For example, during one coaching session, Yasmin, one of Germaine's players, read a short description and set of promised outcomes for a new sales seminar that she'd designed. Germaine asked the player whether she'd buy a book with the same description.

Yasmin said unequivocally that she would. Germaine then asked, "So, by when will you have the book written, Yasmin?"

Yasmin laughed, "I should've seen this one coming. How about by this time next year?"

Further...

d. Ask questions versus tell or advise – Given our commitment to our player's development, we prefer to ask players questions that encourage them to design their own actions and solutions to problems. And given our tendency to tell rather than ask, we have to monitor ourselves.

e. Thunderbolts! Insights – These are recorded for future use. If there are no occasional Thunderbolts! or insights, this may signal that we could design questions that probe deeper or open new perspectives.

f. Other indicators – As previously stated, this section is for measures that we may want to use for this particular coaching session or new ones that we've invented and will want to use ongoingly.

Summary

The Coach's Value model is a remarkably revealing tool. Coupled with meaningful measurements for our coaching effectiveness, it can help us keep our coach/player relationship viable. Aware of the inevitable value drift, we can anticipate it and manage it in a variety of ways. Armed with a Coaching Call Plan Checklist, we can ensure coaching continuity and continually monitor and improve our coaching ability.

Nearly every time we have ever presented the Coach's Value model to anyone familiar with coaching, they have said something like, "You know, coaches really need to examine the player's value as well." We believe this, too, and that is, in fact, the focus of our next chapter.

Chapter 10

Take a group of ten players. The top two will be super motivated. Anybody can coach them. The next four, with the right motivation and direction, will learn to perform up to their potential. The next two will be marginal. With constant attention, they will be able to accomplish something of value. The last two will waste your time. We...focus on the middle six. They are the ones who most need and benefit from your direction, monitoring and counsel.
—Bill Walsh, retired head coach, San Francisco 49ers.
From the Harvard Business Review

THE PLAYER'S VALUE

Outcomes of this chapter:
- Learn more about your players.
- Gain perspective to achieve better results.
- Discover how to let go and move on.

You've seen how the Coach's Value model can assist you as a coach. Here's the complete story: In this chapter, we'll focus on the Player's Value. The model you'll soon understand is a valuable part of your coaching toolkit. We've used it successfully as a way to gain perspective regarding how to better benefit the player/coach relationship.

As you can see in Figure 11, this model is the reverse of the Coach's Value model. It assesses the player.

The Player's Value model is used after a period when you've been coaching players.

Germaine met Paul Bennington at a labor/management conference in Nashville. Paul had been a coach for some time, yet something was happening he didn't understand. Paul said, "I'm wondering if I'm making a difference with my players. I leave the coaching session feeling drained and in a conundrum about what to do with the player."

Figure 11.

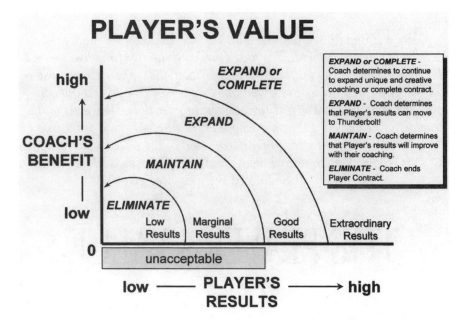

Germaine took a few minutes and did some one-on-one coaching with this coach. She explained the Player's Value model and said, "Once you grasp this concept, you'll be able to sort out for yourself whether a player is worthwhile keeping as a client. The answers are different for every coach and every player."

Take note, whether you're coaching a business team or a team of volunteers, it is necessary for coaches to evaluate the players to determine whom they will keep on their roster and whom they will let go. To do that, the coach must stop, sit down, and evaluate the players carefully. Maintaining players or clients who consistently achieve unacceptable results, for instance, can be unhealthy for the coach as well as the player.

For example, a successful coach and friend of ours, Jane Horowitz, had a client who consistently was delinquent in his monthly coaching payments. She told Germaine, "He's notorious for not keeping his word."

One month, Jane asked her client, Ben, if he had sent the payment in, and Jane said that without a bit of hesitation he replied, "Yes."

A week went by and Jane still did not receive the payment. The mail is sometimes slow, but the client's office was only five blocks from Jane's.

Once again, she called Ben only to find out that the check had not really been mailed. Feel her frustration yet? Many of us have been in this situation, and it's not pleasant. Finally, after the third phone call, the check was mailed, and Jane received the payment two weeks after the due date.

During our coaching session, Germaine asked Jane if Ben was having problems with his clients and creditors in regard to financial integrity. "Of course!" was Jane's reply. "I've had tons of coaching calls with him, and they haven't made a difference."

Germaine asked, "Is it upsetting you that Ben makes his payments late and doesn't tell the truth? Is it worth the hoops that you're jumping through?"

Jane thought about it for a moment and said, "No." She completed her coaching relationship soon after, alleviating herself of the anxiety and making room for a new client. In fact, two new clients materialized within two weeks.

That's a tough decision that we, as coaches, must make at some point in our coaching career. Is it worthwhile to keep a player just for the money when the relationship is not working, as was the case with Jane and her slow-paying, untruthful client, Ben?

> And there comes a time when one must take a stand that
> is neither safe, nor politic, nor popular.
> —Martin Luther King, Jr.

The hard truth is this: You may not be the right coach for a player. Why? You're just not making a difference with the player. The next truth is this: It may be time to step down as coach and give the player up. This takes a lot of courage. You wouldn't be coaching if you didn't think your work was effective, so in a case like this, you may have to admit you're not making a difference.

As a professional coach, you will have to give up potential income when faced with this situation. When we must relinquish a player, our livelihood is jeopardized. However, sometimes keeping a player is the source of the real damage.

The Player's Value model is a great tool to help you delineate the benefit of the coaching relationship with specific players. In a nutshell: It lets you see if the player holds value to you.

Let's take a closer look at the model. An overview of the model is that it compares the player's results to the coach's benefit. It shows just how effectively the coach is impacting the player's results. We've categorized the model into *four* areas: expand or complete, expand, maintain, and eliminate.

Expand or complete: If a player falls in this area, it's because the player produced extraordinary results. The coach determines to continue to expand unique and creative coaching or decides to complete the coaching contract. Should you continue coaching this player, you may want to raise the ante. Become creative with your contract, perhaps including some form of bonus based on performance.

Expand: When the results are good, the player falls into this category. He or she is producing results. You may determine that the player's results can move to Thunderbolt! Perhaps with a nudge, or all-out cheering-section motivation, you can move this player to incredible results.

Maintain: In this sector, the player is producing marginal results. After consideration, the coach determines that the player's results can be improved with coaching.

Eliminate: The player who falls into this section is producing low, unacceptable results. Upon examination, determine if you're the right coach for the job. It may be that the player is uncoachable. It might be that he or she isn't committed to producing the result. Another option is that the player wants to be coached, but the player isn't supported by the company or environment. Here, we recommend that the coach communicate with the player, end the contract, and move on.

Let's imagine that some of your players produce marginal results. Would they be better off with different coaches? Consider that you may be better off without "busting your pick" trying to help them.

One of our colleagues, a professional business coach named Joseph Kenny, says he "cleans house" every six months or so. That is, he looks at his player roster and eliminates a couple of players/clients, assisted by the Player's Value model. Joseph says, "Every time I do this, it somehow opens up my creativity. In addition, the eliminated players are replaced surprisingly fast with new clients." He adds, "It's kind of eerie, really. Every time I let go of two clients or more, the phone starts ringing with prospective clients. Suddenly my coaching schedule is full again. Almost immediately."

When a person works from integrity, this happens like clockwork. Please trust us on this.

The Player's Value model is an excellent tool to check out your integrity as a coach. Try it out. Take one of your contracts out and track the results your player is producing. Now, compare it to the Player's Value model. Are you living up to your contract? Is the player getting value from your coaching? How do the results show up on the model?

Share It—
Sharing the Model with the Player

Let's say you're in an indecisive place with a player, and you're not sure whether you want to continue coaching that person. Share the model with the player; it's simple and straightforward. Ask the player where he or she falls on the model. We've used the model to open the tough conversation about whether the coaching relationship is working. From the dialogue with your player, it'll become evident as to the direction you both need to go.

You can also use the model in the contracting stage. The model gives a potential player a heads up on what can possibly happen during the coaching engagement. It's up to you to assure potential players that should they ever get to the unacceptable areas, low and marginal results, you'll have a dialogue regarding the source of the problem. Yes, this is a courageous step, especially when you're beginning as a coach. However, doing so will assure your potential player that you are a person of high integrity, and that's the coach the player will hire.

> *Success...seems to be connected with action. Successful men keep*
> *moving. They make mistakes, but they don't quit.*
> —Conrad Hilton

Letting Go Is Hard to Do

Have you ever worked on a project where the process keeps you awake at night? If you're a coach, have you ever been so committed to your player's success that you couldn't sleep well? Were conversations always revolving around the project or coaching client? Welcome to our world. Sometimes as coaches, we are so consumed by our latest client that everything else in our world becomes miniscule.

Recently, in Little Rock, Arkansas, we coached a team of executives and a reengineering team that reported directly to the executives. The two teams were a partnership working together; however, the executive team made final decisions. As time went on, the reengineering team became more committed to reaching their original goals than the executives. This was an odd situation to coach. Of course, we tried everything that we've talked about, including the Coaching Spectrum. We wondered out loud, more than once, "What do we do now?"

When we used the Player Value model, we realized that the reengineering team was in every category of the model. They went from producing extraordinary results in some areas to producing low results in others. Definitely, we wanted to continue working with this team.

On the other hand, the executive team was in the same place. Yet, for business reasons, they were dwindling in their commitment to reach the Thunderbolt! results on which they had previously aligned.

Equipped with this insight, we took two different approaches when coaching the two teams. We needed to have both teams on the same page. Our work with the executive team enabled them to see where they were forfeiting their commitment to Thunderbolt! results. They were sending out mixed messages to the team and the rest of the organization. In the end, the executive team recommitted to the Thunderbolt! results and everyone was on track again.

During that coaching engagement, there were times when we had to disconnect. We had become consumed with that client. Each individual reacts differently in a situation. Germaine, for example, talks incessantly to Jed about the possibilities of what she could do. Jed, on the other hand, engages in conversations with everyone he encounters, especially Germaine, about his current project.

If this has happened to you, know you're not alone. As coaches we sometimes get too wrapped up with a client's situation. It's amusing or ironic, perhaps, to think that players rarely know how much contemplation and dialogue we sometimes do on their behalf.

Ingenuity, plus courage, plus work equals miracles.
—Bob Richards,
Olympic Gold Medal winner and minister

When we are steeped in our clients' situations and wrapped up in thinking only about what to do next, we lose sight of the big picture. When this happens, it's best to disconnect. We're not advocating to think about your client only when you are in his or her presence. Simply, when you become consumed with your player and he or she is your only source of conversation, work, fun, etc., it's time to disconnect. Go to a movie, enjoy your family, read a book, do something to relieve your mind of your client.

Great ideas appear when we're relaxed. Then you can go back into the coaching situation with renewed vigor and enhanced creativity.

Summary

There comes a time when you would do well to review your players and the impact your coaching is making. The Player's Value model is an innovative tool to help you decide whether you should move forward with the client or end the relationship.

As we have mentioned, the dialogue you have with players is where the action is, or where you really can make a difference with them. Indispensable to effective coaching dialogue are the questions coaches ask. In the next chapter, we explore how to design questions to open the floodgates of possibility for your players.

Chapter 11

*When observing nature, what we see is the universe exposed
to our own method of questioning.*
—Werner Heisenberg

QUESTIONS COACHES ASK

Outcomes of this chapter:
- Learn the incomparable value of the question as a coaching tool.
- Review the different types of questions that coaches can ask to assist players.
- Extend your coaching ability by discovering how to invent questions to empower your player in the achievement of their goals.
- Re-examine the What, Why, How, Who and When coaching questions.
- Be exposed to a reliable series of questions designed to help understand your players' businesses and objectives.
- Acquire questions to determine your players' personal effectiveness.
- Discover a questioning technique to enhance your players' creativity, to multiply possible actions in order to accomplish their objectives.
- Create new solutions with the ridiculous answer technique.

*Authority is not power; that's coercion. Authority is not knowledge;
that's persuasion or seduction. Authority is simply that the author has
the right to make a statement and to be heard.*
—Herman Kahn

Individual questions, or a series of questions, are the tools smart and effective coaches use. We ask plenty of them and hope you will, too.

Who Is the Master Here?

Effective coaches are masters of influence without authority.

Even where the coach has authority, he or she must wield it intelligently, which often means sparingly, to inspire maximum player performance. Yet, coaches behave in a way to give sufficient direction while allowing players to fully express their thoughts, ideas, and perspectives.

The coach's most potent tool in this regard is the question. But not just any question. The question should open innovative ways of thinking and new fields of possibility. Questions can produce new avenues of action and new options for players. Effective coaches are masters of crafting questions that reveal to their players new pathways to achieve their objectives.

Here's Another One— Types of Questions

There are two forms of questions: closed interrogatives and open interrogatives. Closed questions require direct "yes" or "no" answers or brief responses of singular content. Here are some examples of closed questions:

- Did you find the book I recommended?
- How many days vacation did you take last year?
- How many employees do you have?
- Do you have a pension plan?
- When did you begin your business?

Suitable answers for the questions are "yes" or "no," a number, or a date.

Open questions demand answers with more content or more information. Open questions supply a much wider range of response possibility. And they require creativity and invention on your part. Here are some examples:

- How did you like the book I recommended?
- Tell me about your last vacation.

- What type of employees do you have?
- Describe your retirement program for me.
- How did you happen to get into this business?

In business and personal coaching, you will find both closed and open questions useful and necessary tools. Add the technique of asking questions to your coach's toolkit right now.

> *The brilliant executive coach is the one who brings out the brilliance of the client.*
> —Nancy Kline, *Time to Think*

Inventions Wanted— How to Invent Coaching Questions

We've said that to be effective the coach must always have his or her eye on the player's desired outcome. It is no different when formulating powerful coaching questions. The distance between the player's current level of performance and the intended objective or outcome provide the coach with raw material to form a pertinent question.

Whether or not your question reveals an opportunity or makes a difference for the player is often a roll of the dice. You've got to be willing to ask a lot of questions, and it may take a while before something positive happens for the player. That something positive will almost always be in one of the following four key areas:

1. new knowledge, such as a new action the player could take, a potential solution to a problem, or a fresh perspective on a critical issue; or
2. new skill; or
3. new or renewed motivation to go the distance in order to accomplish the objectives; or
4. new confidence or self-reliance to get the job done.

> *Only when your aspirations and desires lie outside your resources does creativity occur, because you have to invent new ways of competing and changing the rules of the game.*
> —C. K. Prahalad, author

The Powerful Five
What, Why, How, Who and When?

Here are five questions that we always find helpful for our players. Use them to discover new possible actions to move your players toward their intended results, their objectives.

- What must happen?
- Why do you think so?
- How might that be accomplished? How else? How else? How else?
- Who will/should/could be the one(s) to do it?
- When must this be accomplished?

The responses will form a plan to help players realize their objectives.

Before you can get the most from this powerful tool, let's look at the purpose and rationale behind each of these questions:

1. What must happen? What specific, interim outcomes should be accomplished in the timeframe to achieve the player's ultimate objective? Depending upon that objective, this could be the next day, week, or month.
2. Why do you think so? Examine the player's reasons for the selection of interim outcomes. Are there more important or more urgent outcomes that have been overlooked?
3. How might this be accomplished? Here, your question generates a dialogue to explore a sufficient number of possible approaches and alternatives so your player can achieve the interim outcomes. What we mean by "sufficient" depends on the importance or difficulty in making the outcome happen. The more important or difficult the outcome, the greater the amount of choices needed to ensure success. Therefore, we may ask this question over and over again until we have exhausted all the known options and have begun to create new ones. (See the Ridiculous Answers technique later in this chapter.) Then our player selects from the list of possibilities appropriate actions he or she will take to achieve the interim or partial outcomes.
4. Who will/should/could be the one(s) to do it? Who is the person or persons to perform these interim tasks or outcomes? Should it be the

player? Or should he or she delegate the action to an employee or request it of a colleague? Perhaps he or she should hire a contractor.

5. When must this be accomplished? By when must each of these interim objectives be complete? Examine the dates a player selects in relation to the final intended outcome. Do they make sense? Will they forward getting the ultimate outcome done on time?

Let me win. But if I cannot win, let me be brave in the attempt.
—Special Olympics Oath

In the Know— Understanding Your Player's Business

If you are a business coach, the very best tool you have to attain a basic understanding of your player's/client's business is your own curiosity. Develop a genuine interest in your client and your client's business.

The following is a cornucopia of useful questions we've collected and tested over the years. (See Exhibit J.) They have helped us to understand our player's/client's business or playing field. We're not suggesting that you ask every client all 32. Some will not be appropriate for all players/clients.

Further, we're not suggesting these are the only questions worth asking. They've proven helpful to us in learning enough about our clients and their businesses to deliver quality coaching. These questions will help you formulate additional questions of your own:

Exhibit J

Useful Questions

1. What are your "key performance indicators?" How are they measured, or how do you know when you are on track or on course?
2. What are the "critical success factors" in each area of your performance? In your industry?
3. What are your standards? What would be acceptable performance, and what would be Thunderbolt! in each area?
4. Could you describe for me how your organization is structured?
5. What is your company's vision three years out? Beyond that?

---

6. To realize the vision, what are the critical success factors?
7. What obstacles or threats might prevent the vision from being fulfilled?
8. What strategies are in place to assist in realizing the vision?
9. What are your personal goals?
10. What are your company's major objectives this year? How do they correlate to your direct accountabilities?
11. What are the key items on your to-do list today? This week? This year?
12. What are the top critical issues you deal with daily? Weekly? Monthly?
13. In the next 12 months, what major opportunities will you have, and what problems will you face?
14. What areas of your business need improvement? By when must these improvements happen? If these improvements don't happen, what will be the consequences?
15. What does your business' growth picture look like during the next year?
16. What do you consider to be your company's major strength(s) or competitive edge? Any major weaknesses?
17. What significant challenges do your competitors face?
18. What challenges your customers?
19. If you could change anything about your company or department, what would you change?
20. How do you think I might help you improve your business?
21. How do you define coaching, and what do you expect from a coach?
22. Have you had coaching in this area before? What were the results?
23. Of all the coaches you've ever had, whether they were business or sports team coaches, who was your favorite, and why?
24. Who is your biggest champion at the executive level? Who do you think might be a roadblock?
25. How does your performance appraisal system work here?
26. How do you become a "goat" around here?
27. Where do you display your objectives and results against those objectives?
28. Who else knows about your objectives and goals? Who else cares?
29. What do you dream about? What are your dreams? Whose dreams are they really – yours, your parents', Hollywood's, your teachers', your boss', your Aunt Thelma's?
30. What must happen in the next three years for you to be proud of your accomplishments?
31. To whom do you report? To whom are you accountable and for what results?
32. Is there any area that I haven't asked about that you'd like discuss?

*Learning doesn't occur by having all the answers but by
living with the questions.*
—Max Dupree

How Players Work and Play

A basic understanding of a player's business is critical to your coaching success. Even more important, we believe, is understanding how your player functions on a day-to-day basis. How personally effective is the player?

Here's a set of questions that helps us get a sense of how our player performs typically, day in and day out.

1. On a scale of 1 to 10, how would you rate yourself in delegation?
2. How effective are you at utilizing outside resources?
3. Do you practice daily planning and reflection?
4. Do you plan from the whole of your life, or narrowly from usually one area?
5. Describe your typical day. Typical week?
6. How creative are you at generating extra time for yourself?
7. Do you find your work environment supportive?
8. Does your home environment support you in achieving your business objectives?
9. Do you often put things off that you know you shouldn't?
10. Do you generally under-communicate or over-communicate?
11. Tell me about the fun you have in your work and outside of it.
12. Do you do things when you say you'll do them?
13. How often do you make requests of others at work?
14. Do you thank people routinely for their good work?
15. Do you tend to complete the projects you start?
16. Do you find that you have enough energy to meet your commitments?
17. What do you do to celebrate your accomplishments? How often?
18. When was your last vacation, and when will you take one next?

When reviewing these questions, did you wonder if you could actually voice them to prospective clients and players? Many coaches have wondered the same thing, especially at the beginning of the coaching/player relationship.

A less threatening, just as effective, approach is to ask your player to take a self-assessment questionnaire. Let your player know that areas of personal effectiveness are the only topics on which the questionnaire is focused. After your player has filled in the blanks, ask: What did you discover about yourself? We have published a booklet for this purpose called the Eagle's View® Inventory. It contains 25 personal effectiveness questions, a second self-assessment and a progress graph. The Eagle's View® Inventory is available through Eagle's View Systems. (See page 219 for contact information or visit www.eaglesview.com.)

> *To know what you do not know, you must GO where you have*
> *not gone, SEE what you have not seen, DO what you have*
> *not done and BE what you have not been.*
> —Joyce Wycroff, author

Why, That's Ridiculous!

Are you aware that there's power in supplying ridiculous answers? Why? How's that? We can hear you asking right now. There's power because you'll receive some serious responses.

Here is an easy way to tap into creativity, and it works with individuals as well as groups. We have used it to great advantage for several years now. Whenever you find yourself and your player(s) bogged down by a problem or obstacle for which you can't seem to find a satisfactory solution, get ridiculous.

Suggest to your player that you will both be playing a game. The purpose of the game is to break up the impasse and unlock problem-solving thinking. Explain that the game is to think of as many solutions as possible for the hurdle at hand.

Like any game, this has rules, which are simple: Any solution is acceptable as long as it is ridiculous, impractical, and unreasonable. That's right, any idea is legitimate in the game as long as it is...

Ridiculous
Impractical
Unreasonable

The game works best when everyone uses a sense of fun and adventure. Here's an example of how the game is played. You might want to offer this as a sample to get your player or team into the excitement of the game:

Here's the problem: I can't get out of bed in the morning.

Ask your player or players to offer all of the ridiculous, impractical and unreasonable solutions possible. Record the answers. We like using a flip chart, if working with a team.

You'll get answers like these:

- Don't go to bed in the first place. Stay up all night.
- Hire somebody to wake you and drag you out of bed.
- When your alarm buzzes, have a mechanical bed throw you out of bed directly into the shower.
- Hook up a chain to your legs that is connected to a pulley system activated by your alarm clock so that it pulls you out of bed onto the floor and straight into the bathtub filled automatically just seconds before your alarm rings.
- Go to bed with a cattle prod tied to your foot so that it is activated when your alarm goes off.
- Have an electric bed sit you up when your alarm goes off so that you can eat a freshly made breakfast which comes on a tray that pops out of the wall under your nose.

Look at the list again. These ideas undoubtedly sound ridiculous, impractical, and unreasonable. However, those ideas that seem wild inside your mind, when examined in the light of day, can actually help implement solutions. From the list, you could develop ideas that aren't so ridiculous, impractical, and unreasonable. In fact, Bill, one of our friends, who did have difficulty getting out of bed in the morning, developed a workable solution from the last idea on the list above.

Here is Bill's solution: "When I go to bed, I put buttered bread in a toaster oven, which is next to the bed. In the morning, just as the alarm clock goes off, the toaster is activated. As I reach over to turn off the alarm, I smell that buttered toast beginning to brown. It's irresistible. Further, as I turn off the alarm, I reach for the thermos of hot coffee I made the night before."

Bill told us that after he's turned off the alarm, he'd be sitting on the edge of his bed smelling the warming toast with a thermos of coffee in his hands. He said, "I couldn't help but open the thermos and pour a cup. I love the aroma of hot coffee." Coffee in hand, seconds later the toaster rings. "I'm up for good then."

In the end, we will conserve only what we love. We will love only what we understand. We will understand only what we are taught.
—Senegalese saying

Players love to play this game, and it always unlocks a super idea or marvelous solution that never would have been suggested without employing the Ridiculous Answer technique. Ordinarily, when we look for solutions to problems, we automatically look for ones that are practical, reasonable, and certainly not foolish or ridiculous. However, this conventional behavior limits our thinking.

The Ridiculous Answer game frees us to think outside of our traditional social limits and constraints. Our natural creativity for problem—solving is released.

A Washington State power company had a recurring problem. Every winter in the mountains, snow and icicles would collect on the power lines. Hundreds of miles of lines were at risk as they stretched, strained, and eventually snapped. It was a frustrating and nearly hopeless situation. Thousands were without power, especially dangerous during raging winter storms. This was an old problem without what seemed to be a viable solution. Actually, as the story was told to our friend Herb Tanzer, the company had put up with the problem for more than 80 years with countless failures in solving it. The loss of time and money, not to mention interrupted power service for customers, was staggering.

But this time the company was absolutely determined to solve the problem and formed a cross-functional team to tackle the problem.

The new team used all the conventional methods of thinking about the problem, yet as hours stretched to days and days to nearly a week, without one satisfactory solution, a hopeless mindset settled in. "Our brains were mush," said a team member who voted to take a break.

While relaxing over coffee, Ginger, a team member and an administrative assistant, joked: "Let's have the bears that live in the woods climb up the poles. They can shake the poles. Then the snow and icicles will fall off our lines." Two or three people on the team chuckled softly.

Then Kimberly, a manager on the team, thought she'd move the joke along and said, "Yes, that would do it. But what do we have to do to get the bears to climb the poles?"

A lineman, George, stopped nibbling a sticky bun and said laughingly, "Hey, I know! We'll put honey pots on top of the poles. Bears love honey.

You've all read Winnie the Pooh to your kids. Why, those bears would climb the poles to get the honey!"

An accountant, Horace, joined in. "But you'd have to have a whole lot of honey up there to attract the bears. Pots like that would have to be very large and heavy, wouldn't they? I don't think it would be possible, much less safe, for linemen to climb up those poles and attach huge honey pots to the tops of the poles."

George replied, "Well, we could get helicopters to set the honey pots down on top of the poles into baskets."

Then Leeann, an engineer and former military pilot, said, "Are you kidding? The vibration from that helicopter would be tremendous! Vibration so great that the helicopters would blow the baskets with the pots right off the poles! Imagine the liability and the wrath of the animal protection agencies."

Ginger was quiet for the longest time and then asked, "Would the vibration blow off the snow and icicles, too?"

Wham! Bam! Bingo! Thunderbolt! A fresh idea was born!

When we heard this story, we were awestruck, too. Ah, those silly games that coaches play often work well.

What happened? Did the power company use the helicopter solution? We're told that it's standard procedure for clearing the power lines today.

Discovery consists of seeing what everybody has seen
and thinking what nobody has thought.
—Albert St. George,
the scientist who first synthesized Vitamin C

EXERCISE:

Locate a problem in your life that you've been putting up with or a problem for which you have failed to find a favorable solution.

Write out the problem here:

_____

_____

_____

_____

_____

List below every ridiculous, impractical and unreasonable solution you can think of for your problem:

- _____
  _____
  _____
  _____
  _____.

- _____
  _____
  _____
  _____
  _____.

- _____
  _____

- _____
  _____.

- _____
  _____
  _____
  _____
  _____.

- _____
  _____
  _____
  _____.

- _____
  _____
  _____
  _____.

- _____
  _____
  _____
  _____.

Read over your list. Now, invent at least one workable solution to your problem inspired by one of the ideas on your list:

_____
_____
_____
_____
_____

The Ridiculous Answer game can be a powerful eye-opener for players and coaches in removing obstacles and solving problems.

Hypothetical questions get hypothetical answers.
—Joan Baez

Summary

The best coaches are masters of influence without authority, and the most influential tool coaches carry in their bag is the question. Questions can clear the way for players to invent their own answers to carry out their tasks. This expands their power with which to tackle the next obstacle and seize the resultant opportunities. Questions empower players to invent their own answers and solutions, thus developing them for future challenges.

Understanding a player's business is essential for effective coaching to occur. Appreciate and empathize with what the player confronts each day regarding tasks and jobs. A series of excellent questions to help coaches ascertain the nature of their clients' work was presented.

Take a few minutes and review the power of asking ridiculous questions. This resource is essential in your coach's toolkit to unlock creativity, and its effect of tapping into players' natural ingenuity is seldom equaled. Having a problem? Try it on yourself first.

Next, we'll share with you a powerful method of inquiry, guaranteed to enable you and your players to establish an even more profound relationship with their work.

Chapter 12

*The world is not to be put in order, the world is in order. It is for us to
put ourselves in unison with this order.*
—Henry Miller

PANORAMA CARD PROCESS MAPPING

Outcomes of this chapter:
- Understand a powerful coaching tool.
- Discover ways to get the most from the tool.
- Learn how to map the as-is and design to-be processes quickly and easily.

Here is one of the most useful tools we have ever used. Open your coach's toolkit and add Panorama Card Process Mapping.

A process is a method or series of steps to produce outcomes, and process mapping is a technique to graphically represent all the steps of a process. For example, one can process map the steps in writing a book. Now let's take this definition of process mapping one step further:

- As-is Process Mapping: The process as it is currently practiced.

- To-be Process Mapping: A newly designed or redesigned process to be performed in the future.

- Panorama Card Process Mapping helps you to understand a player's business as well as give a player an eagle's view of his or her business processes. Having this information allows the player to see if changes will help to reach objectives. Although process mapping is ordinarily done with teams, it can be done just as effectively with even a single entrepreneur.

Here's the Background

Nearly every type of popular, contemporary organizational change program prescribes process mapping as one of the important steps in a transformation scenario. From elementary Process Simplification to comprehensive Reengineering, all utilize process mapping. Don't get bogged down with those formats. We're giving background so that you're aware of traditional methods.

Those traditional methods of process mapping range widely in length of time to build process maps. Two to three months and two to three days are not unreasonable ends of the time length spectrum. This is partially due to the variety of industries engaged in mapping, the depth and detail required for the process map, and the relative ease or difficulty of access to information that's required to complete the mapping.

Traditional process mapping methods are inefficient:

The tradition of beginning the process map at the start of the process and working through to the end forces an inside-the-organization-out-to-the-customer view of the process. This is less desirable and ultimately less effective than a from-the-customer-into-the-organization perspective.

Drawing and redrawing steps of the process linearly on flat pieces of paper are cumbersome and time-consuming. All of the team members have to wait and watch each step as it unfolds linearly, wasting precious brain power and productivity.

You do what you can for as long as you can; and when you finally can't, you do the next best thing. You back up, but you don't give up.
—Chuck Yeager,
first airplane pilot to break the sound barrier

A Thunderbolt!

We have invented, then polished, a technique that results in a dramatic decrease in the time required to produce the vital process map. It works in all industries. This method has proved itself in redesigning everything from factories to worldwide distribution systems, from global oil and gas company operations, to national sales and customer service systems.

In most cases, the as-is process maps can be completed within only one day. Additionally, to-be process mapping is usually completed in 20 percent of the time traditionally required and with improved quality.

We know there may be terms and concepts that are new to you. But it'll be crystal clear in a moment, whether you're coaching a dentist in new client procedure, your entire corporation, or your teen with techniques to help do well on the SAT.

The Technique's Objectives

- Shape a team environment that fosters innovation and creativity.
- Dramatically increase team members' participation in process mapping.
- Eliminate the waiting-to-be-heard syndrome continually experienced in traditional process mapping methods.
- Improve the quality and substance of the to-be process map, and enhance its implementation.
- Significantly reduce the time invested to produce process maps.

Mapping the As-is Process

After the particular process to be mapped has been determined, the process mapping team is given about 100 panorama cards (we recommend using 3-5/8-inch square cards, available through Eagle's View Systems; see page 221), two flip-chart pages, a six-foot conference table, cellophane tape, and pens. The typical Reengineering, Work Redesign, Process Simplification, or Process Improvement Team is five to eight members. Therefore, each team member will have about 12 to 20 panorama cards and a pen. The two flip-chart pages are laid and taped end-to-end on the table, and team members arrange themselves around the table with their pens and cards.

One team member calls out a step, part, action, or outcome of the process to be mapped. The team member writes it on a card and places it in the center of the table on top of the flip-chart pages. Another team member does the same, then another, and another until all the parts of the process that the team members can think of have been exhausted. Team members call out loud what they write on the cards to avoid redundancy. No discussion of the steps is allowed during this part of the technique. (You'll want to assure your players that they'll have time for this later.) The mood or tone of this part of the technique is freewheeling and chaotic. The things that team members call out will stimulate/trigger information from the minds of the other team members.

After the team cannot think of additional steps other than those on the cards, the members gather on the same side of the table. They begin to arrange, from the pile of cards they've created, the steps of the process represented by the cards in chronological order. Sometimes the team discovers that they are attempting to map more than one process. When this happens, two or three parallel lines may be formed culminating at a finished outcome or set of outcomes. In some cases, there will be disagreement about how parts of the process are performed, in which case further research may be appropriate.

Team members will come up with process steps that were forgotten during the initial "mind dump" and add them to the evolving map. Additional details will be drawn in as required. Within about an hour, 80 to 90 percent of an as-is process map will be complete. The cards are then taped onto the flip-chart pages, and the map can be posted onto a wall.

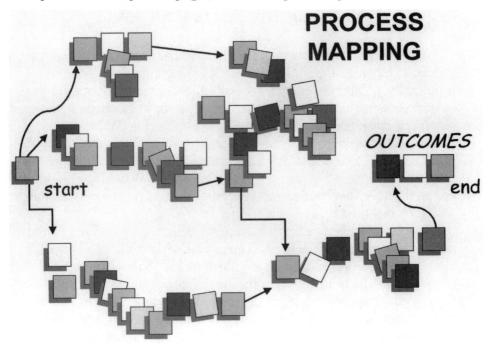

Figure 12.

Designing the To-be Process

Like the method in the as-is process mapping, team members have 12 to 20 panorama cards and a pen. They arrange themselves around the flip-chart pages at the table.

One team member calls out a proposed or possible step, part, action, or outcome of the new process, writes it on a card and places it in the center of the table on top of the adjoining flip-chart pages. Another team member does this, then another, and another until all the proposed parts of the new process that the team members can think of have been said. Again, team members say aloud what they are writing on the card to avoid duplicate ideas. No discussion of the proposed steps that people call out is allowed during this part of the technique, as this happens later. Here, too, the mood or tone of this part of the technique is fast-paced and frenzied.

After all the proposed steps have been written on cards, the team members gather on the same side of the table. They begin to arrange, in chronological order, the steps of the new process. Trust us—lively discussions are the norm. Suddenly, new ideas are brought forth, and the to-be process map begins to take shape.

Additional details will be drawn in as the display evolves and within about an hour or so, 80 to 90 percent of a possible to-be process map will be complete. Cards are now taped to the flip-chart pages enabling the new map to be put up on a wall.

One of our clients, Mike Tate, is a management consultant and coach in Alabama. After we'd shared the Panorama Card Process Mapping method with him, Mike called one afternoon. His voice sounded like he'd just won the Irish Sweepstakes and been awarded a Nobel prize.

Mike had just applied this technique with one of his clients, a team at a local hospital. "The first process the team I was working with chose to map was their patient admissions procedure. They mapped out the as-is process and discovered that there were 96 steps. Then they created a new, streamlined to-be admissions process with only 15 steps. And they did it all in about two-and-a-half hours. Remarkable."

Mike said they were nearly dumbfounded when they fully appreciated the accomplishment and what it could mean to patients and their families. (Mike was, too, but he said he didn't let on how excited he was.)   As you might imagine, Mike's value as their coach climbed up a notch. They attributed their success to Mike and referred him to another hospital in Georgia.

Incidentally, as a side benefit, Panorama Card Process Mapping happens to be a great team-building exercise.

Summary

Techniques similar to the Panorama Card Process Mapping can be effectively applied to plan the implementation of the redesigned processes.

In this chapter, you've learned a procedure to aid both coaches and players to get the big picture. With the map, which is fun and easy to implement, you and your players can see the true nature of their work.

In the next chapter, we offer still another tool. This device helps to widen and deepen your vision. This tool provides players and coaches with a new dimension of the player's world. We call it the DreamMakers & DreamBrakers.

Chapter 13

When working on a problem, I never think about beauty. I think only of how to solve the problem; but when I have finished, if the solution is not beautiful, I know it is wrong.
—Richard Buckminster Fuller

DREAMMAKERS & DREAMBRAKERS! AN EAGLE'S VIEW OF LIFE

Outcomes of this chapter:
- Acquire a new coaching tool that helps coaches and players to get an eagle's view of their lives in relation to their objectives and goals.
- Learn how minor adjustments in one's environment can dramatically improve results.
- Discover how this new tool can launch an ongoing dialogue to assist players and coaches.

Open your coach's toolkit and get ready to add a tool that turns on the power for your clients, your players, and anyone who wants to succeed at anything.

Here's One Audit You'll Want to Have

Here is a simple but highly effective coaching tool. It helps give the total picture for the player and the coach. It's the DreamMakers & DreamBrakers Audit. We explain it to players this way:

Have you ever been 35,000 feet above the planet, soaring safely toward your destination and wonder, How does this enormous bird called a jetliner stay airborne?

The answer, in non-technical terms, is careful management. To fly, there must be a management of the four forces of flight: weight, lift, drag and thrust. Well before takeoff, the pilot or a technician checks the plane's weight to make sure it's within the airplane's specifications. Too much weight and he or she knows that the plane may not be able to generate enough thrust to attain the speed necessary to produce enough lift to takeoff safely.

Once aloft, the pilot vigilantly monitors the instruments in the cockpit to maintain the right amount of thrust, lift, and drag for each of the plane's maneuvers. Too much thrust and she'll fly higher than the designated altitude. Too much drag? She won't be able to sustain the necessary airspeed required to reach the destination on time. Not enough lift and the plane won't fly at all.

The Four Forces of Flight

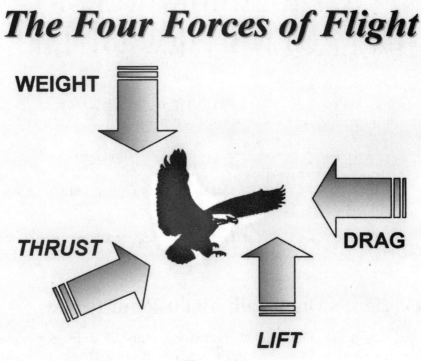

Figure 13.

Now, imagine these four forces of flight as a metaphor, a metaphor for the forces at work in your life.

Wouldn't you agree that to some extent, you are the pilot of your life? As the pilot, you must be in charge to realize your dreams. You must manage the things in your life that drag you down and hamper your speed. You've got to add fuel to the things that provide you with thrust or energy. You try to reduce the things that weigh you down and seem burdensome so you can take off and fly. And you had better surround yourself with enough lift to stay aloft and inspired on the journey to achieving your dreams.

Ironically, the same technological miracles that shrink vast distances and speed complex transactions have left many of us feeling our days are shorter, our to-do lists longer, and the demands placed on us ever more difficult to meet. In a jet, we know we are soaring at incredible speeds, 500 or 600 miles per hour, yet we feel gracefully and comfortably suspended in midair.

In our lives, by contrast, we may feel as though we're moving at a hundred miles an hour, yet results sometimes argue that we're really standing still. All around us, we hear, Fix that problem! Close that deal! Taxi that child! Handle that chore! Why wasn't this done?

At the end of the day, we're often left to wonder why, with so much running around, so little seems to have gotten done. No matter how fast we pedal, it seems as though there is always something tugging at our heels that keeps us from becoming fully airborne.

If dreaming is all your subconscious desires coming out, why do people wait 'til they're asleep to do it?
—Max Headroom, *The Max Headroom Show*

Those "somethings" tugging at our heels are the DreamBrakers. (See Figure 14 on page 145.)

Study the DreamBrakers for just a moment: What keeps you from soaring through life? What's holding you down from reaching your destinations at the speed of light? What comes to mind? Are there weights holding you back?

Let's look a bit further into the forces that allow airplanes and eagles to stay aloft and compare them to the forces that make us feel too rushed or jammed.

Nearly a hundred years ago, Orville and Wilber Wright successfully mastered the four requisite forces of flight when they attached a gasoline engine and propellers to a glider. They called it The Flyer. For twelve seconds, the Wright brothers gained dominion over the air.

Those twelve precious seconds opened up the possibility of human flight forever. These early aeronautical engineers knew they had to overcome the weight of the pull of gravity and the drag caused by the resistance of air to a moving body. They accomplished this by introducing lift (an upward pull produced by wing design) and thrust, (the pulling force provided by the engine and propellers). We call lift and thrust the DreamMakers.

An eagle in flight sees a big picture of the world below. The eagle uses its remarkable eyesight to survey the whole landscape, yet it can zero in on one small moving object, even something as tiny as a field mouse.

The following exercise will allow you to take an eagle's view of your life by conducting an audit of the places in your life where you find weight, lift, drag, and thrust. The simple exercise allows you to take in the whole landscape of these four forces in life and lets you assess which areas could use some adjustment or coordination.

EXERCISE:

Get Ready to Fly

Now, try it yourself. Start by dividing a piece of paper into four quadrants or take out four panorama cards, preferably utilizing four different colors . You may want to write on the form in this book at the end of this chapter. Label the cards or quadrants as follows:

Lift	Weight
Drag	Thrust

Now, in each quadrant, make note of elements in your life that remind you of that label. Here are a few questions to help you along in this inquiry:

LIFT (DreamMakers): What do you find uplifting in your life? What gives you feelings of exhilaration, freedom, and unreserved joy? What makes life worth living? In this quadrant, you might list spirituality, humor, or expressions of gratitude. You might include people who inspire, love, and care for you. You may recall incidents of giving or receiving recognition, or just plain having fun.

DreamMakers & DreamBrakers
(the four forces of flight)

LIFT

Things you find uplifting, such as spirituality, humor, giving and receiving love or appreciation. Things that give you a boost or sense of exhilaration, buoyancy, freedom & joy. Fun.

WEIGHT

Things that weigh you down. Heavy burdens. Things you are resigned to. Obligations you wish you didn't have. Deadlines that seem impossible to meet. Guilt. Resentments.

DRAG

Things that hold you back or impede your progress. Things that provide frustration, annoyance or boredom. Negative complaints. Needless bureaucracy or cumbersome rules.

THRUST

Things that propel you, provide urgency & momentum. Being supported, making requests. New knowledge, insights. Physical energy.

Figure 14.

How about music? How about an engrossing hobby or volunteer activity? How about your animal companions? Our dogs, Lucy and Gus, are a source of joy and wonder for us.

Lift could be provided by watching a movie that you love to see time and again, reading a poem, hanging out in a vacation spot you adore, visiting a spiritual retreat, or reading an inspirational book. Lift is what brings you sheer happiness.

WEIGHT (potential DreamBrakers): What elements in your life do you experience as weighty? Are there things that dominate or oppress you, leave you with a sense of burden, resignation, or perhaps a feeling of being bound?

What takes the air from under your wings? What stops you from flying?

These might be heavy obligations you wish you didn't have, deadlines that seem impossible to meet, lingering guilt over things you should or shouldn't have done, resentments or issues, or events that seem damaging or unfair.

Remember, this is your private list. You need not share this, so please feel free to unburden your weight. Yes, items may seem insignificant to someone else, but if it's weighty for you, please list it here.

DRAG (potential DreamBrakers): What things in your life do you experience as a drag? What are some areas that hold you back, impede your progress, or increase your frustration at every step of the way? Needless bureaucracy or cumbersome rules often make it into this quadrant. Fuzzy objectives can drag you down as you fritter away hours and days figuring out what you ought to be producing. Junk mail, fruitless complaints, defensiveness, antagonism, petty conflicts, and negative interactions are aspects of life that can drag us down. These drags make us feel as though we have one foot nailed to the floor.

THRUST (DreamMakers): Urgency can produce thrust. Urgency gets us into action. What things in your life provide urgency or add a jolt, spurring you to act swiftly and effectively? What things give you a boost?

Completing something can create thrust. It's not just the sense of satisfaction from achieving what we set out to do, but there is freedom available in acknowledging honestly what isn't done. Both are forms of completion. Being complete includes acknowledging what progress has been made, and it even includes acknowledging goals you've chosen to abandon for the moment.

Completion creates an opening in time, a means of transforming time from a constraint to a resource, and an opportunity to act. Thrust is produced from experiences of being supported by others, the ability to make requests of others, and new insights that grant fresh perspectives on issues we face. It certainly comes from being respected and loved. Physical energy provides thrust.

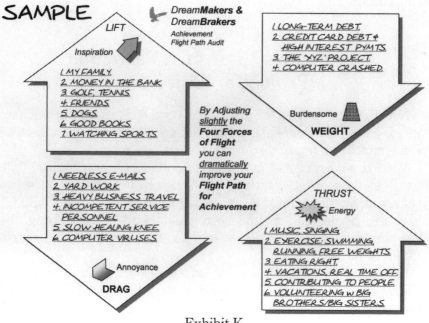

Exhibit K

Take a Good Look

What elements of your life would you adjust in these quadrants?

When you have completed this "audit" of the four forces of flight, you will be ready to take a look at perhaps making some changes to affect the balance of the quadrants. The audit will help get your plans and dreams off the ground.

First, look at weight. What is one thing you can do to reduce unwanted weight? Which element can you reduce, eliminate, or in some way alter so that its impact on you is diminished or even disappears?

Now look at how that single change impacts the other three quadrants. You may find that an action which eliminates weight simultaneously increases lift.

Continue looking. What can you do to increase lift? Look at the things that are dragging in your life. What pulls on you? What annoys you? Can you eliminate something there? Will it allow you to add anything to quadrant four, thrust, that lets you focus your energy toward a specific result? How has the overall balance of the forces in your life shifted by the end of this process?

Get Closer Now—
An Eagle's View of a Particular Project or Objective

Now that you've tried the audit once, try a most useful variation on this exercise. Focus on a particular desired result or single objective. Within minutes, you may discover a solution.

Write down a dream or major outcome that you would like to fulfill. In each of the four quadrants, list the things that can get you closer to your dream or are keeping the dream, or goal, harder to attain. Continue, as above, by looking at the correlation between identifying the DreamBrakers that add weight or drag and the DreamMakers that provide lift or thrust.

What are two, three, or perhaps four simple actions you could take to accelerate the movement toward achieving your goal? Write them down now.

You've got to take the initiative and play your game.
In a decisive set, confidence is the difference.
—Chris Evert

Small Works Well—
Minor Adjustments Equal Dramatic Improvements

If you've attended flight school, you know that one of the first things student pilots learn is to make slight, minor adjustments to the controls to fly the airplane. You learn quickly that gross steering of the wheel and heavy pushing of the pedals, as you do to drive an automobile, are not at all appropriate for flying an aircraft. You have to learn not to work so hard.

Have you ever had the glorious opportunity to watch eagles soar? Have you noticed how these creatures make dramatic turns by only slightly moving the tips of their wings?

It is so of the DreamMakers & DreamBrakers Audit, as well. Don't try to get rid of every ounce of weight or sense of drag all at once. Don't do everything there is to do to improve thrust and increase lift all at once. It isn't necessary. Take it easy.

Change just one, two, or three things in the total of the four quadrants, and dramatic improvements will be made in your "achievement flight path." Be sure you are specific about the changes you decide to make, and set a date by when you will make or start each change. The more specific you are, the greater your odds for completion.

Select changes for which you have control or have the power to make happen. For example, "Have my boss stop yelling at me by Thursday" probably isn't something for which you control the outcome. "Walk a mile three times a week starting today" is in your hands. You have the power to make this happen.

Exhibit L

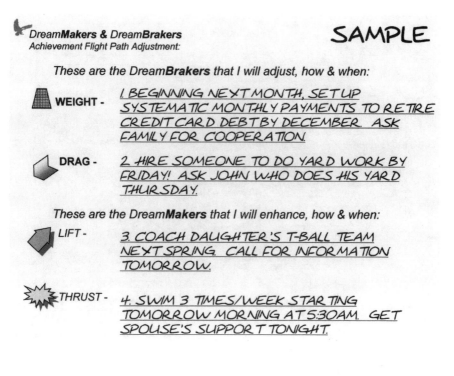

DreamMakers & DreamBrakers
Achievement Flight Path Adjustment:

SAMPLE

These are the DreamBrakers that I will adjust, how & when:

WEIGHT - 1. BEGINNING NEXT MONTH, SET UP SYSTEMATIC MONTHLY PAYMENTS TO RETIRE CREDIT CARD DEBT BY DECEMBER. ASK FAMILY FOR COOPERATION.

DRAG - 2. HIRE SOMEONE TO DO YARD WORK BY FRIDAY! ASK JOHN WHO DOES HIS YARD THURSDAY.

These are the DreamMakers that I will enhance, how & when:

LIFT - 3. COACH DAUGHTER'S T-BALL TEAM NEXT SPRING. CALL FOR INFORMATION TOMORROW.

THRUST - 4. SWIM 3 TIMES/WEEK STARTING TOMORROW MORNING AT 5:30AM. GET SPOUSE'S SUPPORT TONIGHT.

Take a thoughtful look at these basics of flight. When doing so, you'll be able to master those DreamBrakers that create weight and drag, and generate the DreamMakers that give you lift, thrust, and freedom for the demands of daily life. Remember, eagles climb high in the air without working too hard. They fly thousands of feet above the ground without flapping their wings at all. They are masters of the four forces of flight. Happy flying.

> *All men who have achieved great things have been dreamers.*
> —Orison Swett Marden, author

More Coaching Tools

We've written the previous section so that you could experience this awesome device firsthand. (See Exhibits K and L) Once you've experienced the value of the audit, you'll naturally share it with players.

Exhibit M

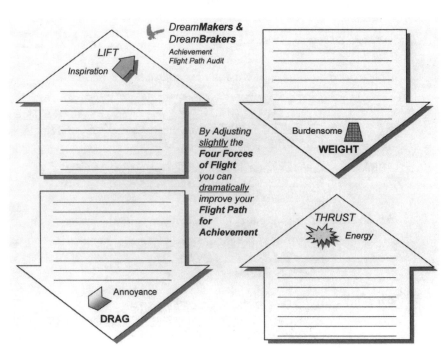

Exhibit N

DreamMakers & DreamBrakers
Achievement Flight Path Adjustment:

These are the DreamBrakers that I will adjust, how & when:

WEIGHT -
_____
_____
_____
_____

DRAG -
_____
_____
_____
_____

These are the DreamMakers that I will enhance, how & when:

LIFT -
_____
_____
_____

THRUST -
_____
_____
_____

We've found this audit to be a rapid way to get to know the people we coach. Even when you've had a long-standing relationship with your player and you think you know him or her well, this audit is bound to reveal useful information that hasn't been distinguished. This tool seems deceptively simple, but its implications to help anyone succeed are enormous. Further, using the audit will help make you an effective coach.

Here is a short description of how we use this unique tool in our CoachLabs and with clients. Please feel free to use our words:

Since most people appreciate the big picture, we always begin by describing the DreamMakers & DreamBrakers Audit. We explain what we mean by the terms weight, lift, drag, and thrust. Then we ask the player, as an assignment, to take 15 to 20 minutes to complete the audit before our next coaching session.

We tell the player that the audit is confidential and that we won't require that any of it is shared. We tell the player that at our next meeting, he or she will be invited to share the audit in a way that the player is comfortable, including actions which might be taken.

The players we've coached are generally quite eager to share with us what they've uncovered during their DreamMakers & DreamBrakers

Audit and the adjustments that they intend to make.

In one of our CoachLabs, Ken and Della, two business coaches from Atlanta, suggested that the DreamMakers & DreamBrakers Audit was too personal a tool to use with their business clients. Della said, "Or at least I wouldn't feel comfortable trying it too early in a coaching relationship." Ken just nodded in agreement.

If you're wondering the same thing, here's our response: While that could be true in certain coaching situations, it hasn't been our experience. We suspect that's because we don't force people to do the audit, and we don't require they share it either. Players, we've found, really get excited about this tool because they often experience their first Thunderbolt! when using it. As we said earlier, we find people eager to share their insights with us. Should a player prefer to not share the audit findings, we are confident that it's still a valuable exercise.

> *Leadership: The art of getting someone else to do something you want done because he wants to do it.*
> —Dwight D. Eisenhower

Leonard Spenser, one client of ours from Dallas, Texas, asked us to coach his wife, Anita, and him in designing their future. We all met at our offices early one Saturday morning.

Always straight to the point, Leonard said, "I'm confused about what to do with my career." He was the local general manager of a large, global consulting firm. He and his wife agreed that he was working too many hours. Although the financial rewards were more than adequate, the year before we met, Leonard had had bypass surgery. They didn't want to risk his health further.

You may know someone like Leonard. You may be in his situation, too. Leonard was considering leaving his company and going out on his own. He said, "I have several issues with my employers I believe need to be resolved."

Anita said, "Naturally, I want Leonard to be happy and healthy," and added that she could "support whatever career path" he took.

After they had painted a general picture of the situation, Jed described the DreamMakers & DreamBrakers Audit to Leonard and asked if he would be comfortable conducting this form of inquiry with all of us present. He said, "No problem. Let's get going."

Jed divided a flip chart page into four quadrants and labeled them weight, lift, drag, and thrust. We proceeded to ask what things came to mind for him in each of the four categories while Jed recorded them on a flip chart. In less than an hour, all of Leonard's uncertainties disappeared.

"This is amazing!" Leonard said. "It's as if a great fog has lifted and a huge weight has just left my shoulders." The audit had given him an entirely new perspective, and he and Anita could see easily their best path forward, which was, in fact, to stay with the corporation, yet use his technical skills to write a book sharing his expertise.

Leonard needed to take a couple of simple, straightforward actions and he would be "flying again." In fact, Leonard has been so pleased with his results that he now uses the DreamMakers & DreamBrakers Audit in his own work with his clients.

Once players complete the audit, we find them referring to the obstacles they face as weights, and any annoyances they experience as drags. This provides an opening to ask them what actions or adjustments they want to make or ask what might be providing any lift or thrust lately.

After the audit, players often start our coaching sessions by saying something like, "Okay, here's my list. Wait 'til you hear the weights and drags. We've got some work to do here."

Periodically, we'll ask players to complete the DreamMakers & DreamBrakers Audit again, without referring to the previous one. They are then asked to compare the two. This provides powerful insights and validation, as well.

Margot Powers, a long-time client in Helena, Montana, said, "So glad I redid this audit. It has shown me how far I've come in such a short time. Before I redid the audit last night, I was in kind of a funk. This thing actually gave me a lift. No pun intended. The things that used to be the great weights have either disappeared or are now just part of life's deal. They're no longer a burden. The things I really enjoy doing that give me lift, I'm doing a lot more of."

Sometimes players do the DreamMakers & DreamBrakers Audit on their own, without being asked and then tell us about it. One of our clients does the audit regularly at the beginning of every month and another player does it every quarter.

The source and center of all man's creative power...is his power
of making images, or the power of imagination.
—Robert Collier, author

Summary

The better you know and understand your clients, the more effective you will be. Find out what's on their minds. What appears to them to be in their way of producing desired results? What things are important to them in life? What turns them off and what turns them on? For a fast, clean method to get the total picture of the player you are coaching, use the DreamMakers & DreamBrakers Audit. It produces meaningful dialogue with players.

Sometime in the future, in a galaxy not so far away, you'll be asked to coach a group of players; yes, a team. In the next chapter, we'll give you some tools to do that effectively from the start.

Chapter 14

None of us is as strong as all of us.
—quoted by Betta Elliott Niederer, author unknown

COACHING TEAMS

Outcomes of this chapter:
- Gain insight into team dynamics.
- Note differences in working with teams and individuals.
- Explore the dynamics of the first meeting.
- Be able to listen to teams more effectively.

Throughout the previous chapters, we've focused on the coaching tools needed to coach individuals. Sometime, someplace, perhaps even today, you'll be called on to coach a team. That's the heart of this chapter. Even if you shake your head and mutter, "No way, no teams for me," we urge you to carefully digest the information. Because, trust us, there are teams in your future.

Everything Changes

Organizational culture has never been static. This is not the corporate world our parents knew or the one we knew just last year. Terms like downsizing, reengineering, process redesign, and participative management are as commonplace as mini vans and double mocha lattes.

Whether functional work teams, cross-functional, task force teams, project teams, etc., people are working in groups. Once a company has been reengineered or downsized, working in teams is often the only way to get projects underway and accomplished.

Below is an overview of how to use the tools with a team.

The more I want to get something done, the less I call it work.
—Richard Bach, *Illusions*

Add This!
The Team Coaching Toolkit

Remember how you learned you were not coachable? This applies to your entire team. Further, you'll quickly discover that the team has a pulse of its own. That's exciting, but if you're new to working with a team, it requires specialized coaching tools.

With teams, you'll be helping them on two levels: as individuals and as the collective group. With team members, you need to know each player's role and who displays leadership on the team. You'll want to educate the team regarding how you coach, your coaching style, and the team's and each individual's style.

In your coaching toolkit, you'll want to distinguish the roles of the team. Why? That's the way you learn about the team's members, who they are, why they are involved.

Are there executives or managers on the team? If so, are there any of their direct-reports on the team? Should there be executives or managers and their direct-reports on the team, you may want to do as we've done. Adopt a ground rule that when working as a team, all players are on the same playing field. This way, people tend to speak out more freely. One exception to this ground rule is when the executive or manager must make a business decision about something that the team is proposing or needs.

You'll need to know: Is the team composed of key people and the right talent for this project? Is there any team member who does not support the successful completion of the project? What are the organizational politics among team members? Is any member vying for the other's job or a specific promotion with the company?

Who on the team demonstrates leadership? This does not necessarily mean the team leader. By leadership, we mean someone who clearly understands and can articulate the goals of the team and impact to the organization. When this person speaks, others listen; rally around his or her ideas.

The leader influences others. Keep in mind that this leader may not be either the manager or the direct report. Yet, he or she somehow influences the people on the team and moves the team forward.

Spend time in talking with the leader. This encourages the leader to focus efforts through the completion of the project. The leader can become your best ally in working with the team. This is also true for those who do not support their team's projects and can cause damage to it in the organization. The leader can become your worst nightmare, too. As a coach, you'll want to make sure that your lines of communication are open with the whole team, leaders, and those with influence, as well.

Most organizations are over-managed and under-led.
—John Kotter, author

Here's How We Do It

When we coach teams, our coaching contract is usually with the sponsor or executive. This person charters the team and may be the team leader. Once our contract is established with the client, we meet with the team. At this point, we review the outcomes with the team and our client ensuring we're all in agreement. As a matter of fact, we have our client write an outcomes contract or charter for the team to fulfill.

Before agreeing to coach a team, review the items in the coaching outcomes contract in the Coaching RoadMap in Chapter 3. Use the Outcome Continuum to assist your client in designing the desired outcomes for the team to produce. Key milestones are set along the way leading to the final objective.

Your neighbour is your other self dwelling behind a wall.
In understanding, all walls shall fall down.
—Kahlil Gibran

No Blind Dates—
The First Meeting, First Session

The first meeting with the team sets the stage. What happens at that juncture can color every future session, including the dynamics of the team, and lays the groundwork to establish you as the coach.

Before the first meeting, take time for yourself. Spend at least an hour alone to clearly identify your goals and objectives as a coach and even memorize a short welcoming speech to share with the team.

During the team's first meeting, do and communicate the following:

- Coaching style and commitment: This is a great opportunity to use the Coaching Scope and the Coaching Spectrum models.
- What the team can count on from you, their coach (expectations).
- Ask permission to be the team's coach. We have each person answer individually rather than collectively. This clears up any confusion later should a player say he or she never agreed on your coaching.
- Design and establish with the team ground rules for working together and with each other.
- Explain (if appropriate) that coaching sessions will be held with the team leader individually throughout the contract, and you will (probably) contact each person for individual discussions. Have an idea of when those meetings will take place because your team members will ask.
- Confidentiality: Explain that you will keep all conversations with team members confidential.
- Allow the team to speak their commitment to reaching their targeted outcomes and milestones.

Throughout the coaching engagement, the coach coaches the team inside the Go the Distance! model in Chapter 2. This is covered in steps 6 and 7: Action/Dialogue & Performance (results) of the Coaching RoadMap. Can you see the dynamics of the Coaching RoadMap?

If we can really understand the problem, the answer will come out of it because the answer is not separate from the problem.
—J. Krishnamurti, *The Penguin Krishnamurti Reader*

Lend Me Your Ear—
Listening to Your Teams

Right about now, you may be wondering, "What about listening? Seems like I'm doing all the talking here."

As we mentioned earlier, when coaching a team, the outcomes must be approved by the executive in charge, often by a team of executives. During one of our engagements with a client, a toy manufacturer in Los Angeles, a session was scheduled with the executives to hear the presentations of work accomplished by 15 teams.

We saw this as a laborious task. Imagine listening to all the teams! While the executives wanted in-depth discussions regarding the teams' findings, we realized it would be frustrating to everyone involved since assuredly the presentations would be interrupted with comments and questions. We knew from experience that most questions are answered as teams report the findings and submit the proposal.

We met with the executive team before the meeting and coached them on how to listen to the teams. They followed our 10 Point Guide. The process went smoothly and stayed on purpose.

You may find this a handy tool to use when working with both teams and individuals.

Executive Leadership Team— What to Listen for During Team Presentations

1. Save questions until the completion of the team's presentation.
2. Are the outcomes achieved in the proposed process(es)?
3. Are you/they happy with the solution/proposal?
4. Watch for handoffs with no responsibility, versus accountability.
5. What's the risk? What is the probability of successful implementation of the proposed changes?
6. Who are the implementers, and when will the implementation be complete? (Are the team members willing to be the ones who will implement their proposal?)
7. Does the proposed work strengthen the company?
8. What are the next action steps for the team to take to begin implementation?
9. Did the team do the necessary research to validate their findings?
10. Are all points of the team's outcomes contract met?

If you compare yourself with others, you may become vain and bitter
for always there will be greater and lesser persons than yourself.
Enjoy your achievements as well as your plans.
—Anonymous

Add These Coaching Tools

The DreamMakers & DreamBrakers Audit described in Chapter 13 (remember the four forces of flight?) is very appropriate to use with a team or individually with team members.

Team members can individually complete the audit and share it with the rest of the team. It's an excellent team-building exercise, and it gets to the source of what is weighing people down in no time at all.

Another use for the audit is for the coach to facilitate the entire team through the audit. The end result is a completed audit that reflects the entire team. From there, the team decides what action steps to take. Try the audit when there's a team overwhelmed by an impasse.

The DreamMakers & DreamBrakers audit works, too, if a team member loses enthusiasm or feels "stuck" on the team. Using the audit, have a one-on-one session with this member to have him or her in action again.

We urge you to experiment with the tools outlined for individual coaching. Remember, Panorama Card Process Mapping is a handy technique to use with teams. Frankie Reece, an HR specialist for a leading bottled water distributor in Northern California, says, "Most team members embrace the brainstorming effect of Panorama Card Process Mapping. It's easy and fun and takes the edge off any nervousness that team members sometimes have when they begin working on a problem. I've seen it supercharge even the most reluctant players because that's exactly what happened with me."

Summary

In this chapter, you've seen how the coaching models are applicable to coaching teams. The tools presented are versatile and can be used easily in conjunction with other tools.

In our next chapter, you'll get a new perspective of a sensitive, powerful, and often misused tool in the coach's toolbox: the telephone.

Chapter 15

*There are two ways of spreading light: To be the candle
or the mirror that reflects it.*
—Edith Wharton, author

COACHING
BY TELEPHONE

Outcomes of this chapter:
- Identify when coaching by phone is effective.
- Explore the advantages of coaching by phone.
- Know when in-person coaching is preferred.
- Enhance your coaching effectiveness by voice mail.

"Good morning, Coaches R Us." That's not exactly what we're talking about when we coach coaches on the use of the phone, but it's a good point of departure.

Many coaches wonder, "Is it really effective to coach by phone?" Our answer? Yes and no.

Between these responses are areas you'll do well to explore. We have discovered there are coaching tasks in which coaching by telephone is preferable to a face-to-face meeting. Conversely, there are times when telephone coaching just won't get the job done.

As with any instruction, sometimes you have to be there to understand what's going on. Many activities require demonstration. Hairstylists, for example, would find it extremely difficult (if not impossible) to learn new hair fashions by telephone. Imagine football coaches teaching players the fundamentals of blocking and tackling by phone.

The generalization, however, that in-person coaching is always superior to telephone coaching is a myth. This may be a Thunderbolt! to you; it has been for many coaches.

Telephone 101

With business going worldwide, the phone is fast becoming an essential coaching tool. It saves time and money. Why then do so many people, professional business coaches among them, have reservations? They think it may negatively affect the quality of coaching. It's a valid concern.

We think it's because most coaches haven't learned to use the telephone effectively. Remember, most of us have never been trained in Telephone 101 past the point of finding the hold button. With some tips, a little practice, and even some coaching, every coach can master coaching by telephone.

May we coach you on the use of coaching by telephone?

For everything you have missed, you have gained something else; and
for everything you gain, you lose something else.
—Ralph Waldo Emerson

Advantages of Coaching by Telephone

1. **The telephone can generate time:** Need more time in your life? Coaching by telephone eliminates travel time. You expend less time and energy. Even if you only have to drive 25 miles each way, if that distance is in Washington, D.C. or Los Angeles, the commute can wipe out half your day. The more you coach by phone, the more room you create for additional clients, tennis, hiking, golf, yourself, and your family.
2. **The telephone is cost-effective:** Assuming that the coaching job can be done as effectively by telephone, it beats the heck out of flying to Toronto from Houston to produce the same result. Contrast a $50 long distance phone bill with roundtrip airfare to Toronto, plus meals and accommodations. What client wants to pay more than 60 times that amount for the same value? If you are not able to bill the client for travel, this part of the equation is more crucial. Further, don't forget the wear and tear on your body. Business travel only seems glamorous to those who don't do it week after week. You know what we mean if you have ever craved a peanut butter and jelly sandwich at midnight while you were 2,000 miles from home, your kitchen, and that jar of peanut butter.

3. **Telephone conversations keep us focused:** People often pay better attention to what's going on in the coaching session while on the telephone. There are fewer distractions. You can get to your point.
4. **We listen better on the telephone:** Effective listening is often enhanced when we don't see the person speaking. Without the visual input, our auditory sense is automatically heightened. We concentrate on, and rely more heavily upon, the content in the language of the player. We take notes while the player is speaking. Who would do that in a casual conversation? We pinpoint whether the player's plans are complete or half-baked. Further, you don't need to see the people to read their feelings. You can hear emotions in a tone of voice. As you coach by phone, remember to coach the dialogue in the pathway to the player's intended results.

Tone of Voice Says It All

When you're on the telephone, players can't see you or read your body language, so the tone of voice is significant. The interpretation of your words is influenced through your voice's tone. If you're up and positive, your player will feel it. If you're experiencing negative feelings or frustration, it collects in your throat and is heard by the listener.

Packard Jennings, a coach in Albuquerque, New Mexico, shared this story: "I was talking with a long-time client about an opportunity to coach a new team and she said, 'Are you okay? You sound kind of down or something.'

"I was surprised she asked because I wasn't aware of any low feelings. Actually, life was going pretty well so I assured her, 'No, no, fine. Really. What makes you say that?'

"She said, 'Nothing really. Well, okay. You just sounded kind of deflated, that's all.'

"It got me to thinking that in person, the clients and the players I coach can see my smile, my facial expressions, but on the phone, I have to work harder on getting that enthusiasm across."

Packard is right. We've noted it, too, and now address this issue at all our CoachLabs. The reason? The telephone, as a mechanical instrument, reduces enthusiasm to the listener. If your tone is up, it won't sound as much so. If you're neither up nor down and just kind of at an even keel, you will sound a little down. If your tone is actually down, you'll sound even worse.

Jed says, "I was taught this early in my former career selling life insurance. I made appointments by telephone. Although I generally contacted those referred by clients, the phone call was the first time I would speak with the potential clients. It's corny, but you never get a second chance at first impressions."

Jed remembers how his agency manager and coach, Dave Thompson, said, "Think of it this way, Jed; there are little parasites in the telephone wires. They gobble up half your smile and half your enthusiasm. So, you've got to be twice as enthusiastic to project how you really are for the person on the other end of that horn to get it."

With this advice in mind, here are some tips to stop the parasites in their tracks:

Stand up: A sure way to get your energy up is to stand up while you are on the phone. In fact, Jed has used a stand-up desk since 1970. He does this to be as alert and high-toned as possible. Coaching on the telephone or doing other work requires a high degree of creative thought. Studies indicate that people think faster and better while they are on their feet. Have your player stand up, too. The call will stay focused.

People can hear your smile: A smile makes such a difference. Put a mirror next to your telephone, and keep it there as a reminder to smile. Should you see a sourpuss staring at you, snap out of it.

Be enthusiastic: To be enthusiastic, act enthusiastic. The rest of you will catch up. Seriously, if you can't muster any enthusiasm for this player or the project, do you have the right to be their coach?

Watch your body: Although the player can't see your body language, you should watch yours anyway. It comes through in your tone of voice. Imagine coaching a player who is hunched over the phone grunting to you. You'd notice it in his or her voice, wouldn't you? Remember, this concept applies to you, too.

> *I just don't want to be hampered by my own limitations.*
> —Barbra Streisand

Listen Up—
What Works by Phone and What Doesn't

What works and what doesn't? Here are guidelines and a little direction. Ultimately, you're the best judge of the effectiveness of telephone coaching. You know the coaching actions to be performed and your players. Right now you probably have a good idea which of your players would find telephone coaching unworkable.

Try this: On a sheet of paper, list all the things that you do as a coach. List the coaching actions you take, the coaching tasks you must perform. This may take a while; you may want to do it over the course of a few days.
1. Go back over your list and put a "T" for telephone. This means that you think or know the task can effectively be done over the telephone.
2. What must be done in person? Put a "P" next to those items. It'll vary from client to client. Write down their names.
3. What things are done even better over the phone? Put a star next to those. This could be a Thunderbolt!
4. Review the P's. Are you sure you have to do those things face-to-face? Consider ways you can have the telephone replace these meetings. Put a check next to those P's that you are willing to experiment with by phone. Make notes on your personal calendar or diary to perform the telephone experiments.

More Modern "Stuff"—
The Modern Technology of the Telephone

To do an effective coaching job, you've got to keep your hands free to take notes. To do so, get a high-quality speakerphone. As Germaine says, "It's no longer necessary to sound like you're at the bottom of a barrel." Some coaches invest in a set of headphones.

Mobile telephones are a great device to keep in touch with your client. We don't recommend a full coaching session while we're behind the wheel of a vehicle. For one thing, it isn't safe. And for another, are you really available to your player when you're stuck in traffic, not to mention speeding down the freeway at 60 mph? Further, you cannot take notes or refer to documents while driving.

Exhibit O

Voice Mail Protocol Checklist

1. Is this the best medium for your message? Do the intended receivers get their voice mail messages frequently enough? Would this message be more effective if written and sent by e-mail, fax, or letter?
2. Before you dial, plan your voice mail message to prevent rambling. Make your goal to be clear and brief.
3. Begin by saying your full name and telephone number slowly and clearly (spell your name, if necessary).
4. Say whether your message is urgent, to inform, a request, a promise, "for your ears only," or an update.
5. Say the number of items or topics this message will carry, and name each topic.
6. Start each part of your message with the bottom line, and then tell the story if it's still necessary.
7. Others listen for meaning (emotional intent) through peoples' tones of voice on the telephone. Think through your message before you send it. Does it convey exactly what you intend?
8. End your call again with your name and phone number. Say if you want a response and by when.

Since the 1980s, the wide availability of advanced technology has enhanced long-distance coaching. E-mail has been assisting our coaching engagements and saves time and energy but will never take away the telephone or in-person coaching. We use the fax machine a lot to share documents and information with players so that, during a telephone coaching session, we can all refer to the same documents, diagrams, graphics, or articles.

Video-conference equipment gives the opportunity to see, speak and connect with one another. Gone are the days of telephone coaching having to be solely an auditory phenomenon.

Dress Up To Look Good and Feel Good

Let's say you have an office in your home; lots of coaches do. The commute consists of walking from the bedroom to the kitchen (for tea or coffee) and then in to your office. Why dress up for talking on the telephone with players and clients? They can't see you, right?

You cannot lounge in your bathrobe and still be an excellent coach. Trust us, we've tried it. We were never as effective. Maybe it was because we just didn't feel up to our game in our pajamas.

When we have a coaching call, we dress professionally. It makes us feel the part. Nowadays, that could include what has become known as business casual. If we know our player is in his or her office in a business suit, we dress as if we are right there sitting in the office, appropriate to the environment. Your dress affects your mood. As we have said, you've got to manage your mood to be at the top of your game. (See Player's Swirl of Moods in Chapter 7.)

> *Planning is everything. The plan is nothing.*
> —Dwight D. Eisenhower

Plan Your Calls Ahead of Time

Don't think you can just wing it on a coaching call. It could be disastrous. Refer to the Coach Call Plan Checklist when preparing for your telephone coaching sessions. (See the Coach's Value in Chapter 9.)

Prepare as if you were meeting in person. For example, if your call is at 8:30 a.m., be there to prepare for it at least 15 minutes before the session. Don't start the call at 8:30 a.m. and try to sort out what you're up to with the player while he or she is on the phone. Take 15 minutes to ask yourself, "What are the outcomes I plan to achieve during this telephone coaching session? What must happen to move this player forward in accomplishing his or her objectives?"

Imagine the intended outcomes having happened. Close your eyes if you must. "How did they happen? What took place to have them happen? What coaching tools did I use? What information did I share that got the job done?" Then quickly get those tools and that information in front of you.

Etiquette When the Call Begins

At the beginning of your call, ask, "How much time do we have?" The answer may surprise you.

Sometimes we believe we'll have an hour, only to have the player respond, "Oh, about twenty minutes." It'll happen to you, too.

It doesn't matter if we've previously established the length of the call, things can come up. This happens with in-person sessions, too. By asking the time question, you will find out how much time you will have at the beginning. Therefore, you won't get "lopped off" at a critical juncture with the player saying, "Oops, gotta run! Bye!"

Knowing how much time you have could restructure your coaching session. You will need to get to the most important topics first or even reschedule the session for a better time.

Thankfully, more often than not, you'll have the time you need. Now, we ask the player, "What would you like to accomplish on this call?" Add these outcomes to the ones brought to the call.

At some point during the initial part of the call, when appropriate, you'll want to say, "May I coach you?" Ask permission to coach. We never take for granted that we are speaking to a coachable player; remember what we've talked about on uncoachable human beings.

Sometimes the call needs to run past the agreed-upon ending time. Ask for more time now or set up an additional call. If you go past the end time unwittingly, as soon as you notice it, acknowledge it and set a new ending time for the session.

Setting an alarm can easily prevent running over time because if you run over and the player knows it (and you don't acknowledge it), we guarantee he or she isn't listening. Can a non-listening player be coached? You know the answer to that one. When this happens, the call has ended. You just missed it and kept talking, unaware that any possible further coaching value had evaporated.

Avoid Telephone Coaching On-the-Run

The best way to perform effective telephone coaching is to be in surroundings specifically designed to support your telephone coaching practice. Avoid attempting to perform quality coaching from airport pay phones or on a cell phone while you're sitting on the commuter train. However, some airports have business workspaces now, and most airline clubs have areas where you can get the privacy you'll need to be an effective coach.

There may be a time in your future when you'll coach from a client's office. When we do, it is always wise to call ahead to make sure we can get the privacy we need. Ask for what you need, including quality telephone equipment with a suitable workspace.

Every day is my best day; this is my life; I'm not going
to have this moment again.
—Bernie Siegel, *Love: The Work of the Soul, Handbook of the Soul*

Take Notes Now, Not Later

Someone once said, "Notes delayed are notes not made." If you're over the age of ten, you've probably found that to be true.

Nearly every time we've been on a coaching call and thought we would have time after to augment our notes, something comes up. Our notes are left incomplete.

To avoid that dilemma, take coaching notes while on the phone and date them. Use a code to flag requests, promises, and decisions made. These are the most important parts of the dialogue. Keep all of your coaching notes in one place, handy for easy reference.

Environment and Organization

Coaching on the telephone demands extra creativity and special energy. When your physical environment is working against you, it consumes more energy, dampens your creativity, and elevates stress. Do you really need more stress? Remember, players hear stress in your voice.

Quick suggestions: Play baroque music in the background. It helps you focus on what you're doing. Coach in privacy, shut your office door, or arrange a time when there will be no distractions. Keep in mind that your coaching sessions are confidential.

Have at hand all the materials and information needed for the call. Focus. Get the clutter off your desk or at least create an unencumbered space from which to coach your player. Straighten up your workspace before you dial the phone. Most of us are unaware just how much clutter adds to stress.

Smile. Return to the section in this chapter on this essential coaching tool. If you don't normally smile when talking on the phone, even to friends, you may have to practice this. It's worth the effort.

Exhibit P

Telephone Coaching Guidelines

1. Have an uncluttered, private workspace and a high quality speakerphone.

2. Dress up – look good and feel good.

3. Prepare the call – what outcomes do you intend for this call?

4. Stand up.

5. **SMILE.**

6. Keep your voice tone up.

7. Ask: "How much time do we have?" Set the call's ending time.

8. Ask: "What would you like to accomplish today on this call?

9. **LISTEN.**

10. Ask: "May I coach you?"

11. Take notes while on the call – not after.

12. Confirm the next call.

Summary

The telephone is a vital and effective coaching tool. It may take some time to master this coaching tool but with the guidelines, practice, and a little patience, you may wonder how you ever doubted that telephone coaching could be effective.

In the next chapter, you'll have the opportunity to add some essential tools to your toolkit that will help design and build a coaching business. Even if, right this second, you're not considering that direction, we hope you'll review the suggestions and recommendations.

Chapter 16

No matter how humble your work may seem, do it in the spirit
of an artist, of a master. In this way, you lift it out of
commonness and rob it of what would otherwise be drudgery.
—Orison Swett Marden, author

HOW TO BEGIN AND BUILD YOUR COACHING PRACTICE

Outcomes of this chapter:
- Design a coaching business.
- Determine the business details that count.
- Learn how to network and promote your coaching business.

Right now your coaching toolkit may seem nearly complete. However, we have a few essential tools you'll still want to add. In this chapter, you'll find tools that are essential for beginning and building your coaching practice.

Let's look at your toolkit and this thing called coaching. Hopefully, the myths and mysteries of this phenomenon have been vanquished. Are you ready for the practical work of "getting into the coaching business?"

For those of you who are interested in beginning your coaching practice, this chapter will get you started in that direction. For those of you who are already in business, you may find some helpful insights. We'll take you through each step that we encountered when we started our business. Let's begin!

Love your work and you'll never have to work again.
—Robert Dale Lindgren, retired successful entrepreneur, Seattle, WA

Get the Blueprints:
It's Time for an Eagle's View!

Let's begin with getting an eagle's view of your coaching business. Refer to the Coaching Architecture on page xx while you're doing this exercise. You will need a large poster size sheet of paper or at least a blank 11 x 14 sheet of paper, crayons or pencil, and baroque music playing in the background.

Eagle's View of Coaching

Figure 15.

EXERCISE:

- Begin by drawing yourself in the middle of the page. You can be as creative as you like. You can use circles, squares, clouds, triangles, whatever. Decide whether you are a one-person coaching practice or if you have associates or partners.
- Next, draw a representation of your clients, or if you don't yet have clients, a prospective of clients. With what type of person do you want to do business? What is your client profile?
- Now, continue to draw everyone and everything you interact with in your business. For example: Under people, you may include attorneys, office assistants, delivery services, vendors, etc. A heading of Technology may include fax, computer, telephones, etc. You'll want to include everything you can that will be in your business environment.
- Include which of the coaching tools presented in this book will be useful for you. From the Coaching Architecture, what tools will you use? Look at your clients and decide which tools, if any, would help you with that particular client.
- Finally, when you have completed designing or drawing your practice, stand up and take a look at what you've just drawn. What do you see missing? It may be a relationship with a banker, or a reliable attorney to work with, or you need to call a client with whom you haven't spoken in a while, or it could even be to put a client agreement in writing. Whatever you find that is missing, begin to make an outcomes list for these things.

With your business designed, let's go back to you. The next two sections focus on your mindset for your business. We believe it's wise to have a clear idea of what your business is about.

*If you want to be a big company tomorrow, you have to
start acting like one today.*
—Thomas J. Watson, Jr., IBM

Why Coaching? Why Not?

Before we go any further, take a moment to answer the above question.

Why coaching? What's calling you to this profession, and why does it interest you? What's in it for you?

We have asked ourselves these questions many times. Coaching isn't all peaches and cream. As we've said earlier, people are uncoachable. You could have Attila the Hun as a client or a Dr. Jeckyl and Mr. Hyde look-alike. Some clients may be weathering the storm for you while others may be créme de la créme. Through it all, you'll hang in there when you have your core philosophy. The why you're in this business makes it worthwhile.

Below is how we answered the above questions.

Remember, as you read them, they're how we responded. You may agree with some of them; others may sound strange to you. The point is, they're ours, and this is what drives us in our business.

What are yours? If you like something here, please feel free to use it.

1. Enable those around us to be successful with less effort.
2. The joy and satisfaction received from contributing to others.
3. Profit both personally and professionally.
4. Earn a good living.
5. The opportunities to live life fully and never get bored.
6. See the world, experience other cultures.
7. Learn from our players/clients.
8. Help end suffering in the workplace.
9. To be fully used up–use all our talents.
10. Meet interesting people and make lifelong friends.

We hope you've gained some insight into why you've chosen or are choosing coaching as your profession. Please jot your reasons down so you don't forget them.

What would you attempt to do if you knew you could not fail?
—Anonymous

Now, Where Did You Put It?
Time to Pull out the Coaching Bio

Remember when we talked about your coaching philosophy and writing a one-page bio? Since you're interested in building a coaching business, it's time to polish it and answer a few more questions.

What qualifies you to be anyone's coach? What's your niche? What are you good at? What is your training and education focus? Are you a health trainer, business coach, relationships coach? Where has your experience taken you?

Begin to make changes to your bio as you answer these questions. Write a brief description of why you're qualified to coach in a particular field and the successes that you've had. You may be thinking that since you are new to this profession and haven't coached anyone yet, you aren't ready to take this step. Hold it right there. We thought that by now you would have changed that conversation. If you're still having these thoughts, reread the introduction and the first four chapters. You may also want to list successes that you've had in your previous work experience.

You may want to dress up your bio by putting a photo at the top of the page or to one side of the bio. You will want to include your office address, phone numbers, e-mail and website address. We have clients who have put their services on the back of their bio. It serves as a convenient tool for their clients and for prospecting. The reverse side of your bio may contain the following business particulars:

- The type of coaching that you do—your particular niche.
- What type of person, organizations or teams you coach.
- Fees charged.
- Products that you offer, including any workshops, personality profiles, etc.

When you've finished dressing up your bio and including everything about your business, give this draft to your colleagues, clients, and friends for their coaching. Teenagers are very helpful with their evaluations, so your best second set of eyes might be living in your house.

Does the bio read clearly? Does it say who you are? Have you included all that you do? How can you improve it? If everything meets your criteria, then it's time to take it to the printer. Let's put it in circulation.

Produce first-class marketing materials for your company. Find an innovative young design team on day one to create a Starbucks/Nike kind of

*feel for the enterprise. [Then put your very own cool image on] every-
thing from the website, to the nameplate, to the business cards.*
—Tom Peters, quoted in Jane Applegate's
201 Great Ideas for Your Small Business

It's in the Details: Business Details

In this section, we're going to talk about business details. You may find some of these things useful.

1. **Fees.** How do you go about figuring what fees to charge your clients? First, look at the type of services that you are offering. Find out what your competitors are charging. One way to find this out is by asking. You will be surprised at what you can find out just by asking. Fees can range from $35 to $350 an hour, for example. Your fees are based on experience, results and the type of work that you do. You may want to publish your fees or not. Look for opportunities where you can receive a monthly retainer from your client with a bonus built in based on results produced because of your coaching. Look to your particular industry and what others are charging for services like yours. Then look at your results, what you bring to the party, and charge appropriately from there. Sometimes it may be worth it to negotiate and ask the client what he/she would be willing to pay to obtain the results they're after. Whatever you agree to, make sure it works for both parties.

2. **Banking relationship.** This is a key relationship to have in business. You'll want to create this relationship for times when business is slow. A good line of credit can rescue your business. If you don't have a banking relationship, we encourage you to cultivate one now. Your business plan will come in handy as you create this banking relationship

3. **Attorney relationship.** Another key relationship to cultivate. You'll want access to an attorney to answer legal questions regarding contracts, trademarks, copyrights, etc. You may even want an attorney to draw up a contract template. We use this type of contract for clients who would like to license our methodology. These contracts are more detailed than the coaching or consulting contracts we use to do work with our clients.

4. **Incorporate.** You may want to investigate incorporating your business. Robert T. Kiyosaki and Sharon L. Lechter, C.P.A., have recently written a couple of books (see our bibliography) about money that may interest you. They mention the importance of incorporating. You may want to talk to your attorney or financial planner about this.

5. **Trademarks and copyrights.** We are believers in having our intellectual property protected through trademarks and copyrights. We respect the work of others and encourage you to do the same. Ask your attorney any questions you may have in regard to these.

6. **Local organizations to join.** You may want to join local organizations as a networking tool so that your business can be listed. Some organizations you may check into are the local ASTD (American Society for Training and Development), your local chamber of commerce, ABWA (American Business Women Association), the Kiwanis Club, and other professional organizations that fit with your expertise. Check your local newspaper or professional journal for an idea of the various organizations and networking groups open to join, such as BNI (Business Network International).

7. **Advertising.** You may want to place an announcement in the business section of your local newspaper announcing your business. This is a great way to advertise and many times, these ads can be done free of charge. If you volunteer in your community or contribute to your community, newspapers are willing to print such stories at no charge. Check out your local cable television station for advertising possibilities. Direct mailing is another way to get your bio and description of services in front of people.

8. **Internet.** Explore the possibility of getting your domain name, website and e-mail. Advertise these on everything that you can.

9. **Stationery and business cards.** Take your time in choosing the design and paper stock for your business cards and stationery. Remember, these represent you and your company. What do you want people to think when they see your business card or receive a letter from you?

10. **Systems.** What systems do you need to put in place? Payroll, accounting, and information systems are a start. Check into possible business software.

Please feel free to add to our list.

Up to this point, we've talked about your mindset, your bio with your business services, and we have taken care of the business details. Now, let's turn our attention to the broad world of networking and getting clients.

> *People today are cynical, savvy, and selective. You have a famous brand? I couldn't care less! You've got three seconds to impress me, to connect with me, to make me fall in love with your product.*
> —Kevin Roberts, CEO, Saatchi and Saatchi,
> from *Fast Company*, September 2000

What Is Your Offer?
What's Your Pitch?

We recommend getting crystal clear about your coaching offer. It will make it much easier for you to build your coaching practice. Get very familiar with saying precisely what you do in six or eight sentences. Write it down and memorize it. Practice saying it in the mirror until the person looking back at you lights up. Practice your facial expressions, too. Say the words with enthusiasm and a smile in your voice. Get that smile to move to your eyes. Then, of course, you'll want to get enough exposure to new people so that you have to say it often.

When we first started our coaching and management consulting, we would invariably be asked the same question every time we traveled: "What do you do?" Almost as soon as we'd get settled in our seats on an airplane, whoever was sitting next to us would ask, "What do you do?" We'd say something like, "Oh, we're management consultants and coaches and..." mostly gibberish from then on. We'd just say whatever popped into our heads. We'd make it up every time.

" 'Arghhh!' we'd later say. This was done in private, of course. 'Why did I say that? Why can't I ever say it so that it sounds good-at least to me? She looked bored. Do you think she was bored? I think she was bored... Heck, I was bored...' "

Know the feeling?

In the beginning, we never thought to prepare for or expected to do any marketing while traveling. That was our excuse and our way to justify being tongue-tied bunglers when it came to our profession. Back then, it was the end of the discussion, although we'll both admit it felt awkward.

Then one day while traveling with our friend and colleague, Mike King, we overheard his answer to the inevitable question: "What do you do?" His answer rolled off his tongue like music. Better still, Mike's succinct and articulate answer actually engaged the other passenger.

After the plane had landed, and while we were waiting for our luggage, we mentioned to Mike how impressed we were with how he described his work and the conversation that ensued. Mike responded, "I've been saying the same thing for 15 years."

This was a Thunderbolt!

It was no accident that it felt like the clouds had just parted to reveal the sun when he spoke it. He'd written it down. Edited it. Edited his edits. Practiced it with his staff and colleagues. Said it in front of the bathroom mirror and the rearview mirror while commuting to work. Memorized it and went out and used it. Mike used it on the phone, on marketing calls, at marketing events, at social gatherings, and on trains, boats, and planes.

"You never know who you'll wind up meeting. It pays to know how to articulate what you do attractively and fast!" Mike said. "Twenty seconds, max. That's all you get. Say it in five or six sentences, or you'll lose 'em."

The luggage carousal turned, and we didn't even reach for our suitcases as Mike continued. "People don't want to hear you fumbling around and groping for words. You don't like to listen to it. Why should they?"

He had us there.

"They sure don't want to hear you getting lost in some long story trying to find your way out." Good grief, now we knew he'd overheard us!

"If what you've got to say turns out to be a little intriguing and the person happens to be someone who could help you, well, you may wind up with a lot more than a pleasant flight home." This was a double Thunderbolt! day. Mike was so right.

We set to work writing our own lilting sentences. We rewrote them and edited each other's edits. We practiced the words until they sounded casual and intriguing. Today when we're asked, "What do you do?" we say this:

"I am co-founder of CoachLab, an international coaching consultancy. We do three things: One, we coach executives, teams, and entrepreneurs; Two, we train people in coaching; and three, we write books about how to coach. Are there things you've dreamt about but haven't found the time? We coach people in realizing their dreams."

Once you've crafted your coaching offer into a few sparkling sentences, you're ready to begin your Networking Adventure.

Why, Why, Why?

Be prepared to answer the following three questions for your prospective clients:

1. Why coaching? (Why would I, the prospect, want or need coaching at all?)
2. Why you? (If I should decide that I'd like some coaching, why should I choose you?)
3. Why now? (Why should I begin a coaching relationship now? Why not later? What's the urgency?)

The answers to the first two questions can be prepared and rehearsed ahead of time. But the answer to the third question is almost always determined during an interview.

Ask questions to uncover what the prospect's dreams and goals are. Ask questions to discover how you might be of assistance.

Decide the amount of energy you are willing to expend to reach your
goal. How many hours are you willing to work a day?
—Les Brown, motivational speaker

Grab Your Backpack, It's Time for the Networking Adventure

Here's one of the best and most natural ways we know to begin to establish your coaching practice.

First, using the form that follows, or one like it, list every person that comes to your mind who might be helpful in establishing your coaching practice. Just write names down as fast as you think of them. Fill in their phone numbers later. These people may be prospects themselves, or they may know people who fit the description of the type of person you'd like to coach. They could be friends, relatives, or acquaintances. They could be colleagues, clients, former clients or people with whom you have done business. List at least 100 names. You'll probably be able to list many more. The more the merrier.

Then after you've finished your list with at least 100 names, fill in their phone numbers.

Now you're ready to call these people.

Name	Phone	Contact Date	Appointment Yes / No	Appointment Date, Time, Location & Notes:
1.				
2.				
3.				
4.				
5.				
6.				
7.				
8.				
9.				

Script #1
Networking Adventure
Request for Referrals

(This script is written for a telephone interview. It can easily be modified for an in-person meeting)

Friend, I'm interested in expanding my coaching practice...and I need your help. Do you have a few minutes to talk now? (If not, make an appointment.) Let me explain what I do or how I work...

(Briefly outline your coaching system and coaching philosophy, unless they are already familiar with it.)

Do you have any comments or questions about anything that I've said? (Give your friend an opportunity to coach you.)

While we've been talking, you may have thought of some people whom I could call. And you may be wondering how I contact people. So, let me just tell you.

I call them on the telephone and say, "Hi, Referral, Friend recommended that I give you a call. I am a professional business coach. Let me assure you, Friend didn't say you wanted to hire a business coach or that you should hire me, for that matter. Friend only said we should get to know one another. Would you be willing to have a cup of coffee with me one day next week, and I can tell you more about what I do?

How does that sound to you, Friend?

Great. So, Friend, who do you know who... :

- is growing their business at a rapid rate?
- is in your firm and is a little stuck?
- could use a strategic-thinking partner?
- just got a promotion or a new job?
- is struggling in their business?
- has a business less than five years old?
- could use a business boost?
- has some management problems?
- dreams of improving their performance but hasn't?
- you'd like to help improve their results?

Friend, I really appreciate you referring me to these people. And I promise to get back to you to let you know how my conversations go with them.

Meanwhile, Friend, let me fax to you my latest coaching biography. It explains a little more about my work and my clients' results. I'd love for you to look it over for me, and I'd appreciate any comments you might have. Would you mind if I called you back in a day or so to ask you what you think of it?

(Call Friend in a day or two and ask for coaching on your biography. Friend may also have thought of some other people whom you should call.)

Script #2
Networking Adventure
Telephone Request for a Face-to-Face Meeting

Hi, Referral. My name is Coach. Friend recommended that I give you a call.

(Allow for anything Referral might have to say about Friend here.)

Do you have just a moment? Great. Referral, I am a professional business coach. And let me assure you, Friend didn't say you wanted to hire a business coach or that you should hire me, for that matter.

Friend only said we should get to know one another. Would you be willing to have a cup of coffee with me one day next week, and I can tell you more about what I do? Or would this week be better, Referral?

(Make the appointment if Referral is willing to meet and if not, thank them for talking with you and end the call.)

Script #3
Networking Adventure
First Face-to-Face Meeting with a Referral

Referral, thank you for taking time to meet with me today. By the way, how much time do we have?

(The answer to that may or may not change how you proceed.)

Great. As you know, I am expanding my coaching practice...and you may find that you're interested in coaching yourself. Or you may know someone whom I should call. Let me explain what I do or how I work:

(Briefly outline your coaching system and your coaching philosophy.)

What do you think so far, Referral?

(Let Referral do most of the talking here. Discover whether Referral might want or need coaching by asking questions like these: (1) Have you ever had a business coach? How did that go? (2) What aspects of your business would you like to improve? (3) Is there anything that you dream of accomplishing but you just haven't gotten started?)

You will find the Questions Coaches Ask in Chapter 11 useful here. If Referral is interested in coaching personally, proceed with your coaching offer. If Referral is not interested personally at this time, proceed as follows:

While we've been talking, you may have thought of some people whom I should call. And you may be wondering how I contact people. So, let me just tell you:

I call them on the telephone and say, "Hi, Referral recommended that I give you a call. I am a professional business coach. And let me assure you, Referral didn't say you wanted to hire a business coach or that you should hire me, for that matter. He only said we should get to know one another. Would you be willing to have a cup of coffee with me one day next week, and I can tell you more about what I do?

How does that sound to you?

(If Referral likes your approach, proceed. Otherwise, ask for Referral's coaching.)

Great. So, Referral, who do you know who...

- is growing their business at a rapid rate?
- is in your firm and is a little stuck?
- could use a strategic-thinking partner?
- just got a promotion or a new job?
- is struggling in their business?
- has a business less than five years old?
- could use a business boost?
- has some management problems?
- dreams of improving their performance but hasn't?
- you'd like to help improve their results?

Referral, I really appreciate you referring me to these people. And I promise to get back to you to let you know how my conversations go with them.

Meanwhile, here is my latest coaching biography. It explains a little more about my work and my clients' results. I'd love for you to look it over for me, if you wouldn't mind. I'd appreciate any comments you might have, Referral. Would you mind if I called you back in a day or so to ask you what you think of it?

(Call Referral in a day or two and ask for coaching on your biography. Referral may also have thought of some other people whom you should contact. Referral may even have decided to take you up on your coaching offer after all.)

I dwell in Possibility –
A fairer House than Prose –
More numerous of Windows –
Superior – for Doors –
—Emily Dickinson, *I Dwell in Possibility*

Pour It On— More Coaching Ideas

We want to leave you with a potpourri of ideas to help you start your coaching practice or build one. You won't want to use all of them by any means. Some, we hope, may just leap off the page at you, and you'll want to do them today. There is no scarcity of ways to promote and build your coaching practice.

45 Ways to Promote and Build Your Coaching Practice

1. Write and memorize a three to five sentence statement describing your coaching practice. Have it be in answer to the question, "What do you do?" Make a game of seeing how many times you can be asked that each week.
2. Write your coaching biography, and always carry several copies with you. Make a game of seeing how many you can give to potential clients each week.
3. Write a one-page description of your coaching practice. Make a game of seeing how many you can give to potential clients each week.
4. Complete the Networking Adventure described in this chapter.
5. Tell everyone you meet what you do, and ask for referrals.

6. Advertise in local newspapers.

7. Advertise on local television.

8. Write newspaper articles about coaching and submit them to local newspapers. (See Bibliography, *The Successful Writer's Guide to Publishing Magazine Articles* by Eva Shaw, Ph.D.)

9. Have local newspapers write stories about you and your coaching business.

10. Do free introductory seminars on coaching and your particular coaching practice. Deliver high value to attendees with a low-key invitation to hire you as their coach. These could be public, private or business presentations.

11. Post flyers in businesses advertising your free seminars.

12. Send letters to selected people you know describing your coaching work, and then call them for an appointment.

13. Fax flyers to people, with a personal note, and then call them for an appointment.

14. Establish a Board of Directors (people whom you've coached or just people who want to see you succeed). Ask them for referrals and keep them informed on your progress. (See Steve Anderson's book, *How to Form a Mastermind Alliance.*)

15. Ask people to write endorsement letters for you and your work, or write them yourself and have people approve and sign them.

16. Collect endorsements of your work by profession and give copies to prospects in those professions.

17. Send postcards to prospects/clients while traveling, and call them when you get home and ask for referrals.

18. Give people a "Who do you know who..." card describing the categories of people you'd be interested in talking to about coaching. (See Networking Script #1 for sample categories.)

19. Join organizations that can help you meet people or introduce you to people with whom you'd like to do business.

20. Get scheduled as a speaker at local associations and groups.

21. Make a list of everyone you've ever known. See what pops out. Call the people who might help you.

22. Make presentations to small business owners.

23. Drop in on business owners and personally invite them to your free seminars.

24. Invite people from whom you buy goods and services to find out

about your coaching work.

25. Go through your business card collection and mail or fax those people your bio and/or one-pager.

26. Select a niché market, such as real estate agents, and do a "multi-touch" campaign. A multi-touch campaign is a series of mailings (or faxes or e-mails or any combination thereof) to the recipients about your work. Then when you call, there's a chance they may recognize your name.

27. Whenever you talk to someone, always give him or her the opportunity to learn about your coaching work.

28. Put flyers up on bulletin boards in buildings and businesses or in the window.

29. Put flyers in people's boxes in businesses.

30. Give a coaching scholarship to a key decision-maker in a target company.

31. Send helpful news or magazine articles to people and follow-up with a phone call.

32. Submit letters to the editor to get your name in print.

33. Invite local newspaper or magazine writers to be in your free seminars. Perhaps they'll write about the seminar and you.

34. Make a list of people that you would like to coach. Then for each name, list five more people of whom they remind you. Then call those people and tell them what you're doing.

35. Send posters to friends/clients advertising your scheduled introductory seminars and ask if they would post them in their offices or businesses.

36. Have a Tupperware-type party for coaching, an in-the-home introduction (and perhaps demonstration) for your coaching practice.

37. Host a party celebrating the grand opening of your new coaching business. Send invitations to people from your Referral Adventure List.

38. Make flyers containing a $25 coupon for your coaching. Distribute to new prospects that you meet with personally and at other events.

39. Read the local newspapers and magazines. Send articles to potential clients about their business with your bio and/or one-pager about your work. Then call them for an appointment.

40. Hire someone to call people and make appointments for you.

41. Get to know the top businesspeople in your community. Discover

what their issues and concerns are and how you might help them. Tell them what you're up to and ask whom else you should meet.

42. Hire a coach to help you build your practice.
43. Read Jane Applegate's book, *201 Great Ideas for your Small Business* and Harvey Mackay's networking book, *Dig your Well Before You're Thirsty*.
44. Rent a booth at trade shows, conventions.
45. Do volunteer work.

Summary

With the tools found in this chapter, you're definitely on your way to designing and building your own coaching business. You may want to try out the scripts and create introductions using words with which you feel comfortable.

Before each race, Olympic gold medal winners and twin brothers Calvin and Alvin Alexander say to each other, "Follow your destiny," instead of "good luck." "Good luck" leaves room for something to go wrong.

So we say to you: Follow your destiny.

In our next chapter, we'll talk about power and patience, tools you'll find useful in coaching and in life.

Chapter 17

Power's footstool is opinion and his throne is the human heart.
—Sir Aubrey De Vere

PATIENCE AND POWER

Outcomes of this chapter:
- Understand the concepts of patience and power.
- Learn how to utilize patience and power for improved coaching.
- Find out how to unplug from coaching when consumed by it.
- Complete a coaching self-assessment.

Throughout this book, we have shared new concepts and models with you to enhance your coaching ability. We have talked about patience and power in the context of other topics; but in this chapter, we'll explore it as the must-have tools included in your coach's toolkit. The final tool we suggest you add is the Coaching Inventory. It's simple and effective.

Patience and Compassion

Remember when we used the example of learning to tie your shoestrings? Can you remember teaching it to a child? You may recall it took a few attempts and practice before you or the person you were teaching finally got it right.

That's how it is when learning something new. How was it for the person who taught you? Whoever it was, it took patience and compassion on his or her part. It took compassion to work through your futile initial attempts. That's how it is with coaching.

Your player may not always understand the concepts that you are offering or the urgency that you feel as a coach. The player may sometimes want to quit.

Successful coaches hang in there, even in the toughest of times. Refer to the Swirl of Moods models that we discussed in Chapter 7. Both players and coaches experience different moods throughout the coaching engagement. If your attention is on your player's mood and what's happening with him or her, you can show compassion and coach unproductive moods or dialogue which are happening.

Sometimes people are more committed to being wrapped up in their drama than getting in action toward the completion of their goals. Simply put, the drama may be more exciting.

It's times such as these that the coach has to be patient to un-stick the player. In athletics, coaches call this intestinal fortitude, or staying with the player until he or she is back in the game. The following is such an example where a team member, Tim Colby, was wrapped up in the drama of why he couldn't get something fixed.

As we coached a team in a manufacturing facility, Tim complained about a safety hazard. Tim explained where and what the problem was in long technical sentences better suited for chemical engineers than business coaches.

Germaine asked, "Tim, what needs to happen to repair the problem?"

Tim looked at Germaine, took a deep breath, and repeated the story all over again. When he finished, Germaine once again asked, "Tim, what needs to happen to repair the problem?"

Tim stared at Germaine and repeated his story once more. This scenario replayed itself about three more times until Tim finally heard Germaine's question.

You see, Germaine saw how upset Tim was and patiently listened. All the others on the team saw what was happening. They patiently watched the dynamics of this one-sided conversation as Tim continued to be unavailable to hear Germaine's question.

Do you ever have conversations like that with players? Whether the players are your children, a group of volunteers, or the employees of your client, the situations occur. Sometimes you are just not heard because the player is too busy playing out the drama. The upset is all-consuming.

Patience is a tool you'll need in your toolkit. You must have patience to free players from the hold of the upset until you can be heard.

By the way, once Tim could finally hear Germaine, he came up with a solution to the problem and got permission to fix it. Later that night, as we were walking to our cars, we ran into Tim. His smile said it all. "I fixed the problem. It could have been really terrible. An accident waiting to happen—guess you heard more than you wanted to today. Right,

Germaine? Now the people who work in that area of the plant will be safe and I can sleep tonight."

Patience in Reaching Thunderbolt!

Coaching the player to reach the intended results and the Thunderbolt! may be a process that's long and arduous. There may be unforeseen problems such as changes in the market, a sudden loss of customers, or a buyout affecting the player's strategy for achieving results. Whatever the situation, the enthusiasm that was present at the inception of the contract has disappeared.

This is one of the moods in the swirl. There will be times when the road to accomplishment is tough. What's a coach to do? From our experience, we recommend you have a coach or a confidant with whom you can communicate. Doing so allows you to free yourself from the negative self-talk that creeps in about your performance as coach or about your player. And sometimes we have to be reminded of our personal commitment as well as the commitment we have to our player's success.

One of our clients went through a bad three-month period in his business. It was a brutal time. There were days when Phillip didn't want to face the world. We changed our coaching routine during this time. Since everything was a burden to Phillip, we decided to free him from the burden and created weekly games with him. We turned drudgery into fun. So, one week the game was to call on X number of clients; the next week may have been to close one project, etc.

Phillip made it through the slump. Both patience and compassion made a difference in our coaching dialogues. We celebrated whenever Phillip scored or accomplished something. The celebration was in the form of an enthusiastic acknowledgment, "Yeah, that's great, way to go!"

> *Give with love, joy, and a sense of fun, and the windows of heaven will be thrown open with a blast.*
> —John Randolph Price, author

Let's Talk About Power

In our consulting practice, we often train employees within a client organization to become internal consultants and coaches. We have observed that midway through training these employees, something always happens. The others in the organization begin to notice that these people are now rubbing elbows with the executives and spending a tremendous amount of time with us.

Not only that, but the trainees begin to speak and act in new ways. Others take notice. Their peers begin to speak to them (the internal consultants) like they have a lot of answers about what's happening in the organization. This is the time when we have to have the conversation about power with the internal consultants and coaches.

What these novice coaches are experiencing is a newfound power within the organization. They are now in meetings with executives, behind closed doors with consultants and coaches. You may have seen this working with players. It's dramatic. The players appear to know things of a confidential nature. Also, their knowledge of being internal consultants and coaches is expanded, and their confidence is ever increasing. And it shows.

Despite all the knowledge they gain and the training provided, they may fail to grasp one thing: awareness of their power. Equipped with the new knowledge and stature within the organization, the internal consultants can no longer enjoy the luxury of being careless about how or what they say to others, especially anything about the executives or the consulting intervention that is taking place.

With their new power comes responsibility. The actions and dialogue of the internal coaches now carry added weight and validity in the eyes of others in the organization. The interpretations they share about their organization will now, more than ever before, move it forward or set it back.

> *Our power is not so much in us as through us.*
> —Harry Emerson Fosdick

Kilowatts? What's This Power All About?

Let's talk about the meaning of power. Below are quotes on the subject of power from people in all walks of life. We ask you to consider these as we look at the phenomenon of power.

I feel it now: There's power in me to grasp
and give shape to my world.
I know that nothing has ever been real without my beholding it.
All becoming has need (of) me...
—Rainer Maria Rilke

Power doesn't corrupt people, people corrupt people.
—William Gaddis

Every man has enough power left to carry out that of
which he is convinced.
—Johann Wolfgang von Goethe

I think that education is power. I think that being able to communicate
with people is power. One of my main goals on the planet is to encour-
age people to empower themselves.
—Oprah Winfrey

Power is the faculty or capacity to act, the strength and potency to
accomplish something. It is the vital energy to make choices and deci-
sions. It also includes the capacity to overcome deeply embedded habits
and to cultivate higher, more effective ones.
—Stephen R. Covey

The miracle, or the power, that elevates the few is to be found
in their industry, application, and perseverance under the
prompting of a brave, determined spirit.
—Mark Twain

Opportunities? They are all around us. There is power lying latent every-
where waiting for the observant eye to discover it.
—Orison Swett Marden

What Does All This Mean?

What does power mean to you? How does power fit in the coaching
relationship? Reading and contemplating the quotes, a spirit of determi-

nate just-do-it attitude, intelligence, and courage emerges. What came to you? Who possesses this power? From the quotes, it sounds like anyone who breathes has the potential to be wrapped in the cloak of power. What if, during each conversation with your players, you listen to them to make sure that they are speaking from a position of power? How would that dialogue sound?

Let's Get Personal

We've talked about this before, but it pays to add a reminder here. You will never be coaching strictly business practices and corporate players even if all you talk about is business. The coaching techniques and tools you share with players will be applied to the players' personal lives. However, should a player ask questions of a personal nature that you morally or ethically cannot answer, speak up immediately. Yes, you'll be asked, so it pays to know what to say ahead of time. Perhaps you'll want to know how to suggest getting some professional therapy or contacting various self-help groups.

On the other hand, don't be shocked when your players report that they're using "your" tools to help their volunteer groups, their kids, and even their own un-office side of life. It's happened to us.

They Have Reasons

Players hire a coach for lots of reasons. Yet, one thing is a constant: the player wants support in accomplishing specific results in his or her life.

A coach sees and hears things that a player doesn't. The tennis coach can see the player's body position when serving the ball. The player cannot. The acting coach who stands at the rear of a theater can tell if the actor's voice carries well, the actor cannot.

As mentioned earlier, great coaches are masters of influence. Influence is power. Coaches have power and we, as coaches, need to be keenly aware and responsible for how that power is used.

Since coaching is built on relationships, players oftentimes look to the coach for answers. Refer to The Coaching Scope Model in Chapter 4 that graphically distinguishes questions and answers. As mentioned there, we lean toward the side of asking questions whenever possible (especially when we're not experts on that business or area).

We do not have all the answers, nor are we interested in having all the answers all the time. We believe the answers best lie within the player, and our job is to elicit the answer from them. That's the job of the coach.

For example, one of Germaine's players, Jill Cortez, was in an ethical dilemma and asked Germaine what she should do. At this point, Germaine could do one of two things: (1) tell the player what to do, or (2) have the player follow her own sense and code of ethics. The first choice is an example of Germaine taking power away from the player, and the second choice is an example of allowing the player to choose what to do, which is powerful for the player.

As a coach, one thing you don't want to do is deprive players of their power and the responsibility that comes with it. You want to be cognizant of how much you are actually directing and leading players in their actions.

Porché & Niederer: Unplugged

This is useful information for both players and coaches. You may want to share this part of the book with your players and your colleagues.

Have you noticed just how much "stuff" you have on your mind? Right now, what are ten of the things that demand your attention, regardless of where you are? Go ahead, name them or write them down. Your list might include these: leaky water heater, client who doesn't return phone calls, the oldest child getting yet another sore throat, finding a new gardener, wondering whether the medical program at work will cover all of your bills, a paper cut, not getting a call from Mr. or Ms. Right, the guilt over an imagined or real problem with a parent/friend/colleague/loved one, mortgage rates, crashing computer programs, weird sounds in the car's engine again, a hurtful comment from an associate, and the ever popular, "never enough time for me." And don't forget: Do you think you're gaining weight?

The stuff we're talking about are the thoughts and moods that inhabit your mind at every moment. These are the things that demand your attention and which can and do rob you of your power. They can constantly pull at you and stop you from enjoying or focusing on the moment you are experiencing.

While you can't toss these worries off the nearest cliff or use them to fuel a bonfire, try to recognize those things that eat away at you and stop you from participating fully in the moment. As you realize what these things are, it is possible to mentally "unplug" from them. Unplug is a metaphor for release.

Picture an octopus with eight arms, each plugged into an electrical outlet. Each electrical outlet represents a thought, mood, or person that zaps the octopus' energy. Imagine that you are in the place of the octopus and the arms represent your energy.

As you unplug, feel the difference. Do you feel whole, complete and powerful again? This is a technique that Caroline Myss, educator and medical intuitive, describes in her work. We approach it with a little different spin.

Germaine likes to do this exercise when she showers. "I begin to focus on what thoughts or moods are clouding my mind. As a thought enters, I imagine being plugged into that thought, and I unplug, demanding my mind to release that situation, person, or mood." By the time she's finished showering, she's feeling light and energetic. Her power comes back.

Jed, on the other hand, gets on all fours and plays with our dogs, Lucy and Gus, to unplug.

Other coaches say they recharge doing the following things:

- Spending time with spouse and children
- Playing with grandkids
- Listening to music
- Walking
- Running
- Reading for pleasure
- Baking bread
- Gardening
- Swimming
- Creating crafts
- Doing yoga
- Watching funny movies
- Cooking
- Washing the car
- Playing fetch with your dogs
- Petting your cat
- Visiting a museum or amusement park
- Volunteering
- Praying/meditating
- Mowing the lawn

Unplugging and then recharging is essential. Find three or four activities that recharge you and include them in your week, every week.

*If you are distressed by anything external, the pain is not due
to the thing itself but to your own estimate of it; and this
you have the power to revoke at any moment.*
—Marcus Aurelius

The Coaching Inventory

We saved one of the best tools for last. It could be the most powerful one in your bulging toolkit. It's the coaching inventory and is applicable whether you're coaching a team from a Fortune 500 company, one-on-one with a client, a kids' golf team, or the scout troop before the cookie sale.

The self-assessment helps target areas of coaching for you to work on, enhances your effectiveness, and improves your players' productivity. It'll give you a "game plan" from which to work while reviewing the models and information in this book.

The inventory is designed to provide possible coaching structures, principles, practices, and approaches while you assess your coaching ability.

How to Complete Your Coaching Inventory

You'll need a block of time from 25 to 30 minutes to complete this self-assessment. It's most effective if done in one sitting.

Rate yourself on a scale of 1 to 10 for each of the 55 questions. Ten is the highest rating. In the Inventory, you'll judge your experience of yourself or your sense of yourself in the area, how you view yourself. Draw a circle around the number on the scoring bar below each question that approximates your self-rating number score. If you score yourself less than a 10, write a note about why in the space below the scoring bar. See the sample inventory questions and answers below.

The Coaching Inventory

SAMPLE QUESTIONS AND ANSWERS

45. I can clearly distinguish coaching from management, leadership and mentoring.

1	2	3	4	5	6	7	8	9	10
Not clearly									Clearly

I have an idea – but not certain.

46. I am conscious of the preferred behavioral style of each player (the person being coached) and calibrate my coaching style, strategy and tactics appropriate to the individual.

1	2	3	4	5	6	7	8	9	10
Unconscious									Very Conscious

Not for my entire team yet.

47. I am clear about the principles and concepts of effective coaching.

1	2	3	4	5	6	7	8	9	10
No Clarity									Crystal Clear!

I want to learn more.

48. My players know my expectations as their coach and I know their expectations of me.

1	2	3	4	5	6	7	8	9	10
They do not									Yes

Some do, and some don't.

Figure 16.

Okay, go ahead and complete the inventory now, and you might want to play some baroque music as you work.

Coaching Inventory
(self-assessment)

Name _____ Date __/__/__

1. The players that I coach are inspired to achieve extraordinary results.

1	2	3	4	5	6	7	8	9	10

No   Inspired

2. I am just as enthusiastic about my players' "wins" as I am about my own successes.

1	2	3	4	5	6	7	8	9	10

Seldom   Always

3. I am confident that I can coach people to produce extraordinary results.

1	2	3	4	5	6	7	8	9	10

Uncertain   Confident

4. I am generally intolerant of excuses.

1	2	3	4	5	6	7	8	9	10

Too Tolerant   Intolerant

5. I am inspired by the people whom I coach

1	2	3	4	5	6	7	8	9	10

Rarely   Frequently

6. Players experience that I am committed to their success.

1	2	3	4	5	6	7	8	9	10

I don't know   Absolutely

Figure 17.

7. I listen for my player's commitments—not just their plans.

1	2	3	4	5	6	7	8	9	10

Don't Distinguish Commitments   Yes

8. I confront difficult situations head-on and diplomatically, rather than avoid them.

1	2	3	4	5	6	7	8	9	10

Avoid Always   Yes

9. I am confident in my ability to effectively coach all the players who report to me.

1	2	3	4	5	6	7	8	9	10

No Confidence   Confident

10. I generate an environment of open and honest communication such that players are not shy about letting me know when they need help.

1	2	3	4	5	6	7	8	9	10

Shy   Forthright

11. I am trainable & coachable regarding coaching and I welcome the opportunity to become more effective in my work.

1	2	3	4	5	6	7	8	9	10

Quite Resistant   Coachable

12. Players leave my coaching sessions energized, with new openings for action, committed action steps and deliverables.

1	2	3	4	5	6	7	8	9	10

Rarely   Always

13. I build strong relationships with my players based upon my commitment to their outstanding performance.

1	2	3	4	5	6	7	8	9	10

No   Yes

14. I listen to fully understand my player's unique point of view before I speak. I am an effective listener.

1	2	3	4	5	6	7	8	9	10

Rarely   Always

15. I plan for and prepare thoroughly for each coaching session.

1	2	3	4	5	6	7	8	9	10

No Preparation   Always

16. I record and follow up regularly regarding what players say they will do.

1	2	3	4	5	6	7	8	9	10

Seldom   Quite Regularly

17. I have a coach myself, and use him or her regularly.

1	2	3	4	5	6	7	8	9	10

No Coach   Use Often

18. Every so often I call a player spontaneously just to see how they are doing or to provide encouragement or coaching.

1	2	3	4	5	6	7	8	9	10

Never   Yes

19. I ask more of players than they would ask of themselves.

1	2	3	4	5	6	7	8	9	10

Never   Often

20. The players I coach accomplish their targeted results.

1	2	3	4	5	6	7	8	9	10

Never   Always

21. I ask permission first before coaching.

1	2	3	4	5	6	7	8	9	10

Never   Always

22. I fully utilize appropriate coaching tools and techniques in my coaching sessions with my players.

1	2	3	4	5	6	7	8	9	10

Don't Use   Fully Utilized

23. Through coaching I am able to expand opportunities for my players to help them improve their results.

1	2	3	4	5	6	7	8	9	10

Never   Frequently

24. When coaching, I err on the side of asking questions versus telling players what to do & how to do things, or providing answers.

1	2	3	4	5	6	7	8	9	10

Tell Mostly   Ask Usually

25. Through coaching, my players commit to taking actions that they would have otherwise never attempted.

1	2	3	4	5	6	7	8	9	10

Seldom   Often

26. When players promise to do something and do not, I don't ignore it or let them "off the hook", but rather I call them to account.

1	2	3	4	5	6	7	8	9	10

Never   Always

27. I limit feedforward to one or two key areas so that my players are not overwhelmed with input.

1	2	3	4	5	6	7	8	9	10

No   Yes

28. I use questions to uncover root cause performance challenges and enroll players in actions to take for their personal improvement.

1	2	3	4	5	6	7	8	9	10

Rarely   Always

29. I keep coaching conversations focused and on track.

1	2	3	4	5	6	7	8	9	10

Rarely   Always

30. I ask probing questions that have players communicating the truth, challenges and fears that may be inhibiting them from succeeding.

1	2	3	4	5	6	7	8	9	10

No   Yes

31. I have regularly scheduled coaching sessions with the players whom I coach.

1	2	3	4	5	6	7	8	9	10

No   Regularly

32. I have a written, strategic coaching plan for each player that I coach.

1	2	3	4	5	6	7	8	9	10

None Written   For Everyone

33. I have written coaching contracts with specific measurable outcomes for each player so that we are clear about what we want to achieve through coaching.

1	2	3	4	5	6	7	8	9	10

None   All

34. I make myself available for impromptu coaching sessions with my players, and they are aware of my availability and how to reach me.

1	2	3	4	5	6	7	8	9	10

Not Usually   Always

35. My players are enrolled in, and have a clear understanding of the vision, objectives and strategies of their organization.

1	2	3	4	5	6	7	8	9	10

They Are Very Resistant   Completely Enrolled

36. I give feedforward in-person and as close to the event as possible.

1	2	3	4	5	6	7	8	9	10

Never   Always

37. I challenge players' perspectives to broaden their possibilities for expanding their results beyond their objectives.

1	2	3	4	5	6	7	8	9	10

Seldom   Often

38. My players are aware that they may call me in between our regularly scheduled coaching sessions whenever they require assistance or just want to talk.

1	2	3	4	5	6	7	8	9	10

Unaware   Fully Aware

39. My players collect and maintain accurate records on their actions and outcomes for the things we are working on together.

1	2	3	4	5	6	7	8	9	10

Seldom   Regularly

40. I coach my mid-range performers for improving and expanding their results and I coach my stars for retention & career advancement.

1	2	3	4	5	6	7	8	9	10

No   Yes

41. I invest monthly 3 to 5 hours coaching each of my players who have written coaching outcomes contracts with me.

1	2	3	4	5	6	7	8	9	10

Never   Always

42. I help players target high-value opportunities for action in their projects and steer them away from low-value activities.

1	2	3	4	5	6	7	8	9	10

Never   Always

43. My players are clear about my definition of coaching and the benefits of an effective coaching relationship.

1	2	3	4	5	6	7	8	9	10

Unclear   Clear

44. I know my players' current objectives in key areas of productivity and I know the past history of their results in those areas.

1	2	3	4	5	6	7	8	9	10

Not Known   Yes

45. I can clearly distinguish coaching from management, leadership and mentoring.

1	2	3	4	5	6	7	8	9	10

Not Clearly   Clearly

46. I am conscious of the preferred behavioral style of each player and calibrate my coaching style, strategy and tactics appropriate to the individual.

1	2	3	4	5	6	7	8	9	10

Unconscious   Conscious

47. I am clear about the principles and concepts of effective coaching.

1	2	3	4	5	6	7	8	9	10

No Clarity Whatsoever   Crystal Clear!

48. Players know my expectations of them as their coach and I know their expectations of me.

1	2	3	4	5	6	7	8	9	10

No   Yes

49. Players know my coaching philosophy.

1	2	3	4	5	6	7	8	9	10

What Philosophy?   Yes

50. My players are committed to their own personal growth and development.

1	2	3	4	5	6	7	8	9	10

No   Yes

51. I understand how to have coaching conversations that assist players in closing the distance between their current levels of results and the level of results they say they are committed to achieving.

1	2	3	4	5	6	7	8	9	10

Unclear   Understood

52. My players are certain about the difference between the *coaching* conversations I have with them and the *management* conversations we have.

1	2	3	4	5	6	7	8	9	10

Don't Distinguish Any Difference   Certain

53. I am aware of my players' dreams and aspirations and how to guide them in advancing their careers or help them grow their businesses.

1	2	3	4	5	6	7	8	9	10

Unaware   Fully Aware

54. I know where my players are investing their time each week and provide coaching when I believe their time to be misallocated.

1	2	3	4	5	6	7	8	9	10

Fully Aware   Unaware

55. I enter every coaching session fully aware that I can enhance every player's performance or reinforce his or her loyalty & commitment to the organization.

1	2	3	4	5	6	7	8	9	10

Unaware   Fully Aware

Total Score: _____ divided by 5.5 = _____%

I plan to improve in the following areas:

_____

_____

_____

_____

_____.

Questions by coaching dimension:
  Being: 1-14. **Practices:** 15-30. **Structure:** 31-43. **Knowledge:** 44-55.

After you have answered each question, total your score for all 55 questions. Now divide it by 5.5 to translate it into a 100 percent scale. Since you applied your own personal standards when you completed this inventory, your scores will not be objectively comparable with other people's scores.

Now, plot your score for each question on your spider progress graph, figure 19, and note the date and total score for this inventory. To assist in identifying areas in which you'll want to pay particular attention, the inventory is divided into four dimensions or categories: **Structure**, **Being**, **Knowledge** and **Practices.** We define these dimensions as follows:

Structure: Organizing for coaching sessions. Composing interrelated parts to form a coaching system or organization to help deliver coaching systematically.

Being: Coaching manner or a "way of being." This is a person's experience of the present, including thoughts and feelings. Mental and physical qualities demonstrated or experienced by a person. It is one's fundamental or essential nature.

Knowledge: Having familiarity, awareness, understanding or education regarding coaching. Having information about the player essential to effective coaching. Possessing principles, procedures and practices of effective coaching.

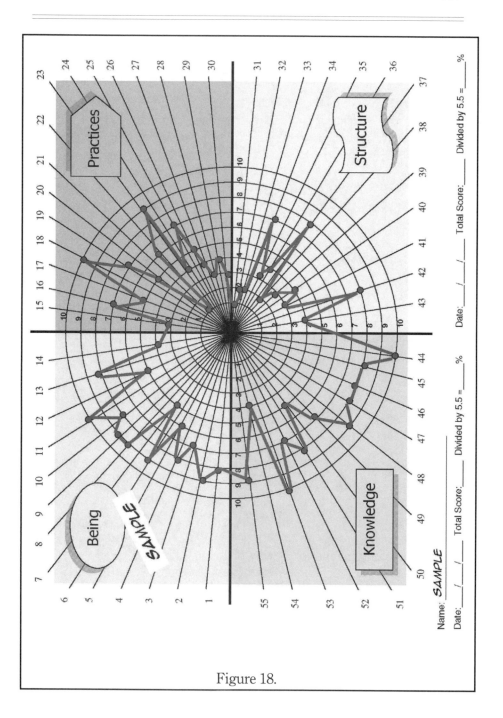

Figure 18.

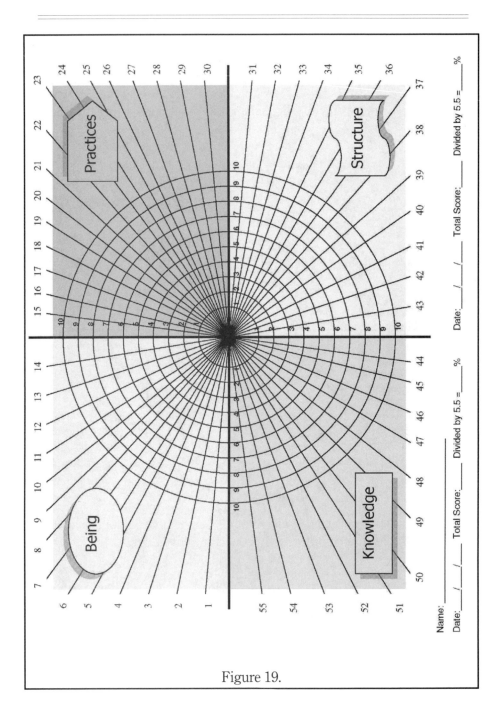

Figure 19.

Practices: Engaging in practical and useful actions regarding coaching. To use one's coaching knowledge frequently. Having proper coaching habits or customs. Repeated performance. To observe or adhere to one's philosophy, standards, beliefs or ideals about coaching. The application of coaching principles results in the condition of being proficient or skillful.

See Figure 18. Notice that this sample spider graph illustrates that the coach's weakest coaching dimensions are structure and practices and his strongest dimensions are being and knowledge.

Results Count

As a result of completing your Coaching Inventory, we recommend that you go back and re-read those portions of the book that can help you address any gaps in your coaching technique. Use the self-assessment as a guide to improve your skills.

Two weeks after reading or re-reading this book, re-take the Inventory and note your progress.

It's been our experience that those who take the Inventory experience improvement in coaching areas important to them. Your scores should improve naturally, just by putting a little attention on the area.

Where your attention goes, so goes your energy. Therefore, just by completing the Coaching Inventory, you may find yourself naturally improving your coaching habits. At the same time the inventory is an opportunity to acknowledge your strengths. This is often an uplifting experience, which may provide a surge of energy for your coaching endeavors. We suggest to you that whether you are new to coaching or you are a seasoned veteran, you have already enhanced your coaching effectiveness just by completing this Coaching Inventory.

Summary

Coaching requires patience. Patience allows the player to communicate fully, and patience helps you bear it all even when the road gets tough. Coaching is a roller coaster phenomenon that allows both coaches and players to experience a swirl of moods during its course. Patience blended with compassion helps the coach contribute to players.

At some point, everyone experiences power. Coaches have the capability of empowering their players or influencing their players to the point of controlling. This is "coach dependency." Our job as coaches is not to rob our players of the freedom of choice, but to encourage and support them to choose.

Successful coaches increase their player's confidence, self-esteem, knowledge, and motivation through their coaching ability. One technique that allows people to become centered, focused, and whole is unplugging. Unplug from the thoughts, moods, and people that are demanding your attention at inopportune times. Remember once you unplug, you'll need to recharge, too.

It has been our privilege in this book to share our work with you. The following quote sums up what we call Thunderbolt! coaching.

Go to the people,
Learn from them, love them.
Start with what they know,
Build on what they have.
But the best of leaders, when their task is accomplished
and their work is done,
"We have done it ourselves," the people will all remark.
—Chinese poem, 23 B.C.

BIBLIOGRAPHY

Albom, Mitch. *Tuesdays with Morrie*. New York: Doubleday, 1997.

Anderson, Steve. *How to Form a Mastermind Alliance*. Hunt, TX: Planned Marketing Associates, 1996.

Applegate, Jane. *201 Great Ideas for Your Small Business*. Princeton, NJ: Bloomberg Press, 1998.

Beckwith, Harry. *Selling the Invisible*. New York: Warner Books, 1997.

Bennis, Warren and Burt Nanus. *Leaders*. New York: Harper and Row Publishers, 1985.

Birkman, Roger W., Ph.D., The Birkman Method, personality profile evaluation, available from the publisher, Birkman Associates, Houston, TX.

Blanchard, Kenneth, Ph.D. and Robert Lorber, Ph.D. *Putting the One-Minute Manager to Work*. New York: The Berkley Publishing Group, 1984.

Blanchard, Kenneth, Ph.D. and Johnson Spencer, M.D. *The One-Minute Manager*. New York: Berkley Books, 1982.

Block, Peter. *Flawless Consulting*. San Francisco: Pfeiffer and Company, 1981.

Block, Peter. *Flawless Consulting*, 2nd ed. San Francisco: Jossey-Bass-Pfeiffer, 2000.

Bly, Robert. *Iron John*. New York: First Vintage Books Edition, 1992.

Brondfield, Jerry. *Rockne*. New York: Random House, 1976.

Cowan, John. *Small Decencies*. New York: HarperCollins, 1992.

Davis, Stanley. *Future Perfect*. Boston: Addison-Wesley Publishing, 1987.

DeBono, Edward. *Parallel Thinking*. London: Penguin Books, 1995.

DePorter, Bobbi. *Quantum Learning*. New York: Dell Publishing, 1992.

DePorter, Bobbi and Mike Hernacki. *Quantum Business*. New York: Dell Publishing, 1997.

DePree, Max. *Leadership is An Art*. New York: Doubleday, 1989.

Dyer, William G. *Team Building*. Boston: Addison-Wesley Publishing, 1987.

Goldratt, Eliyahu M. and Jeff Cox. *The Goal*, 2nd ed. Boston: North River Press, 1992.

Goss, Tracey. *The Last Word on Power*. New York: Currency, Doubleday, 1996.

Hall, Edward T. *Beyond Culture*. New York: Anchor Books, Doubleday, 1976.

Hammer, Michael and James Champy. *Reengineering the Corporation*. New York: HarperCollins, 1993.

Handy, Charles. *The Age of Unreason*. Boston: Harvard Business School Press, 1989.

Helgesen, Sally. *The Female Advantage*. New York: Doubleday, 1990.

Hudson, Frederic M., Ph.D. *The Handbook of Coaching*. San Diego, CA: Jossey-Bass Publishers, 1999.

James, Jennifer. *Thinking in the Future Tense*. New York: Simon and Schuster, 1996.

Kerr, Michael E. and Bowen Murray. *Family Evaluation*. New York: W. W. Norton, 1988.

Kiyosaki, Robert T. and Sharon L. Lechter, CPA. *Rich Dad Poor Dad*. New York: Warner Books, 1998.

Kiyosaki, Robert T. and Sharon L. Lechter, CPA. *The Cashflow Quadrant*. New York: Warner Books, 1999.

Kline, Nancy. *Time to Think*. London: Ward Lock, 1999.

Koch, Richard. *The 80/20 Principle*. New York: Currency/Doubleday, 1998.

Kriegel, Robert and David Brandt. *Sacred Cows Make the Best Burgers*. New York: Warner Books, 1996.

Lee, Robert J., Ph.D. and Arthur M. Freedma, Ph.D. *Consultation Skills Reading*. Arlington, VA: NTL Institute, 1984.

Lippitt, Gordon and Ronald Lippitt. *The Consulting Process in Action*, 2nd ed. San Diego, CA: Pfeiffer and Company, 1986.

Mackay, Harvey. *Dig Your Well Before You're Thirsty*. New York: Currency, Doubleday, 1990.

McCarthy, Kevin. *The On-Purpose Person*. Colorado Springs, CO: Pinon Press, 1992.

McCormick, Charles P. *The Power of People*. New York: Penguin Books, 1985.

Myss, Caroline, Ph.D. *Anatomy of the Spirit*. New York: Three Rivers Press, 1996.

Myss, Caroline, Ph.D. "Three Levels of Power," audio edition of the PBS television special. Boulder, CO: Sounds True, 1997.

Naisbitt, John and Patricia Aburdene. *Megatrends 2000*. New York: William Morrow, 1990.

O'Keeffe, John. *Business Beyond the Box*, 2nd ed. Nicholas Breasley: London, 1999.

Oriah Mountain Dreamer, *The Invitation*. San Francisco: Harper San Francisco, 1999.

Orsburn, Jack D., Linda Moran, Ed Musselwhite, and John H. Zenger. *Self-Directed Work Teams*. Chicago: Business One Irwin, 1990.

Pascale, Richard Tanner, *Managing on the Edge*. New York: Simon and Schuster, 1990.

Pascale, Richard T., Mark Millemann and Linda Gioja. *Surfing the Edge of Chaos*. New York: Crown Business, 2000.

Pritchett, Price. *Teamwork*. Dallas, TX: EPS Solutions, Change Process Practice, Pritchett and Assoc., Rummler-Brache Group, Dublin Group, 1992.

Rapaport, Richard. "To Build A Winning Team: An Interview with Head Coach Bill Walsh," *Harvard Business Review*, 1993.

Reddy, Brendan W. and Kaleel Jamison. *Team Building*. Arlington, VA and San Diego, CA: NTL Institute and University Associates, 1988.

Schein, Edgar H., *Process Consultation*, Volume 1, 2nd ed. Boston: Addison-Wesley Publishing, 1988.

Scott, Dru, Ph.D. *The Telephone and Time Management*. Menlo Park, CA: Crisp Publications, 1988.

Shaw, Eva Ph.D. *The Successful Writer's Guide to Publishing Magazine Articles*. Loveland, CO: Rodgers & Nelsen Publishing, 1998.

Silbiger, Steven. *The Ten Day MBA*. New York: William Morrow, 1993.

Tanzer, Herb. *Your Pet Isn't Sick*. San Diego, CA: Wharton Publishing, 1999.

von Oech, Roger. *A Whack on the Side of the Head*. Menlo Park, CA: Creative Think, 1992.

Weisbord, Marvin R. *Productive Workplaces: Organizing and Managing for Dignity, Meaning, and Community*. San Francisco: Jossey-Bass, 1991.

Wheatley, Margaret J. *Leadership and the New Science*. San Francisco, CA: Berret-Koehler Publishers, 1994.

Zander, Rosamund Stone and Benjamin Zander. *The Art of Possibility: Transforming Professional & Personal Life*. Boston: Harvard Business School Press, 2000.

BIOGRAPHIES

Germaine Porché and Jed Niederer have also co-authored *Volume 2, Coach Anyone About Anything: How to Help People Succeed in Business and Life*; the bestselling book series *Coaching Soup for the Cartoon Soul; The Power of Coaching: The Secrets of Achievement; The Power of Coaching: Managing the Time of Your Life and the CD series, Ask The Coaches*. They are the creators of CoachLab® and the Eagle's View® time transformation workshops.

Germaine enjoys running marathons, yoga, strength training and bicycling. She finds relaxation reading, cooking food of all kinds and spoiling her nieces and nephews. Jed enjoys chi running, cartooning, reading and appreciating classic automobiles. They both love traveling together and volunteering for youth mentoring programs. Germaine and Jed have been married 21 years and reside in Houston, Texas with their dogs Gus and Mitzie.

Germaine V. Porché, MSOD

Germaine specializes in working with organizations to produce performance breakthroughs in productivity and leadership. She coaches executives and groups at all levels to achieve their commitments. Germaine provides individual coaching in productivity, leadership and personal effectiveness to executives, entrepreneurs and families on their interpersonal relationships. She is a resourceful and innovative designer of consulting interventions. Germaine is President and co-founder of Eagle's View® Systems, Inc., Houston, Texas, USA.

Her 20-year consulting has included work in the energy, manufacturing, forest products, sales, insurance, customer service, law and real estate industries. Germaine has delivered her work in the United States, Canada, Europe, Indonesia and Israel. She has an outstanding history as a sales and marketing professional. Prior to entering the consulting profession, she founded a realty company and built a reputation for expert knowledge and top service.

Germaine holds a masters degree in Organizational Development (MSOD) from The American University in Washington, DC and the NTL Institute (National Training Laboratories). She earned a B.A. in Management at Our Lady of the Lake University, San Antonio, Texas.

Edward "Jed" Niederer III, CLU

Jed has coached executives, managers, teams and entrepreneurs to break-through performance for 30 years. A skillful program developer and deliverer, Jed has created and led courses and workshops in personal effec-tiveness, communication, leadership, sales and coaching for more than 100,000 people in the US, Canada, Europe, The Far East, Middle East, South America, and Australia.

Jed's consulting and coaching career has included work in mining, manu-facturing, energy, insurance, computer, forest products and healthcare industries. He is a co-founder of Eagle's View® Systems, Inc. Jed has suc-cessfully managed projects involving a wide range of large-scale change methodologies including Rapid Work Redesign, high-impact work teams, and breakthrough process reengineering.

After earning a B.A. in Communications & Advertising from the University of Washington in Seattle, Jed entered the life insurance business and became a million-dollar producer his first year. At age 24 he was appointed the youngest-ever agency manager for Provident Mutual Life eventually leading his associates to win the President's Trophy. Jed holds a Chartered Life Underwriter (CLU) degree from The American College, Bryn Mawr, Pennsylvania. He served as a Second Lieutenant and pilot in the US Army Transportation Corps.

Coaching Tools & Models Index

Here is a great reference tool for you – a list of every coaching tool or model we've described in this book and where to find them.

INDEX